John Lowry

Negotiation Made Simple

A Practical Guide for Solving
Problems, Building Relationships,
and Delivering the Deal

HARPERCOLLINS
LEADERSHIP

AN IMPRINT OF HARPERCOLLINS

Published by HarperCollins Leadership, an imprint of HarperCollins Focus LLC.

Any internet addresses, phone numbers, or company or product information printed in this book are offered as a resource and are not intended in any way to be or to imply an endorsement by HarperCollins Leadership, nor does HarperCollins Leadership vouch for the existence, content, or services of these sites, phone numbers, companies, or products beyond the life of this book.

ISBN 978-1-4003-3633-3 (eBook)
ISBN 978-1-4003-3632-6 (HC)

Library of Congress Control Number: 2023942872

Printed in the United States of America
23 24 25 26 27 LBC 5 4 3 2 1

To my dad, Randy Lowry, who taught so many,
including me, how to negotiate effectively,
efficiently, and respectfully.

CONTENTS

Foreword by Donald Miller vii

Introduction: Getting Started—Life as a Great Negotiator xi

Part I
Manage Yourself

CHAPTER ONE: You Are a Negotiator 3

CHAPTER TWO: Strategy Wins 11

CHAPTER THREE: Success Starts with You 25

Part II
Ambitious Competition

CHAPTER FOUR: The Characteristics of
     Competitive Negotiation 47

CHAPTER FIVE: Master Your Most Important Move 61

CHAPTER SIX: Concede with Purpose 77

Part III
Creative Cooperation

CHAPTER SEVEN: Transition from Positions 95

CHAPTER EIGHT: The Roadmap to Resolution 113

CHAPTER NINE: The Power of Empathy 121

Part IV
Deliver the Deal

CHAPTER TEN: Prepare for the Process 135

CHAPTER ELEVEN: Overcome the Obstacles 151

CHAPTER TWELVE: Know the Secrets of Satisfaction 169

Conclusion: Make a Difference One Move at a Time 185

Acknowledgments 187

Appendix: Negotiation Made Simple Self-Assessment 191

Your Next Steps to Making Negotiation Simple 197

Notes 199

Index 211

About the Author 217

FOREWORD

Years ago I attended a John Lowry negotiation training in which John taught me and about twenty other business leaders several negotiation principles that, unbeknownst to me, would make and save me millions, keep me out of court, create better relationships with friends and family, and even make me a more confident business leader. To be honest, I wasn't expecting to get so much out of the course. At the time I didn't think I negotiated all that much but I had recently started a company and was trying to round out my leadership abilities.

The weekend after I took the training I saved $800 on a used riding lawnmower. A few months after that I saved $800,000 on a piece of land. Within a few years I owned equity in several small businesses and, more recently and more importantly, my two-year-old will now drink from either the blue sippy cup or the red sippy cup regardless of whether Mommy is with us. That was a big one, but, using John's principles, I got the job done.

I went into the training thinking that learning to negotiate would be like learning jujitsu, that I'd have to brace myself for psychological combat. But that's not what happened. Certainly there are negotiations that feel a lot like a battlefield game of chess, but most of the time negotiation is really just about recognizing the context you are in and responding with an appropriate counter move. After John's training, negotiation felt more like a dance to me than any kind of combat.

I gained so much from John's class that I asked him to teach an on-demand course for my small business platform. That course was so liked by small business owners that I asked if he'd be willing to put his thoughts down in a book. You're holding the book.

This book is going to be helpful to you not just once, but more likely every day for the rest of your life. Just recognizing the two types of negotiation and understanding which negotiation you are in could make or save you millions and also keep you from being trapped by a bully on a tear.

If I were in your shoes, I'd read this book carefully. I'd read it twice, in fact, and then I'd read it again with a highlighter in hand while listening to the audiobook. The principles in this book are as much about human psychology as they are about negotiation, which means this book will help you understand the motives and workings of others, which is a skill that will contribute to your success like few others.

Some of you might be asking, "Hey Don, how did you get such a skilled negotiator to film a course and write a book and share his knowledge with the world in such an accessible way? Wouldn't he be better off selling this information to individual clients for millions in the context of high stakes negotiations?

Yes, he would.

But I used his own tactics against him without him even knowing it. And now we all benefit. How's that for negotiation, John?

You are going to love John and you are going to love this book. Enjoy.

DONALD MILLER
CEO of Business Made Simple and author
of *How to Grow Your Small Business*

INTRODUCTION

Getting Started—Life as a Great Negotiator

Every teacher once was a student. Every winner once was
a loser. Every expert once was a beginner. But all of them
crossed the bridge called "Learning."

—ANONYMOUS

There's a story about an old farmer, his neighbor, and a carpenter. It's been told in different versions by different people
over the years, but it goes something like this: There was an
old farmer who lived on a farm and was close with his neighbor for years. Both of the farmers' spouses had passed on, and
all they had left was each other and their farms. One day they
got into an argument about a stray calf. Each claimed to be the
owner of the calf. They couldn't settle the dispute, and their
stubbornness began to kick in. Full of resentment toward each
other, they stopped talking altogether. This went on for
months. Years of friendship went down the drain because of a
single calf they both thought belonged to them.

One day a traveling carpenter showed up at one farmer's
door looking for work. The farmer invited the carpenter inside
and had him look out the window toward his neighbor's farm.

He told the carpenter the long story about how he and his neighbor used to be friends, but they were no longer talking because of their disagreement over a calf months ago. He pointed out the creek that separated their farms. He instructed the carpenter to build him a tall fence along the creek so the separation of the farms would be clear and complete.

The farmer purchased the lumber and piled it up next to the creek, and the carpenter went to work. The farmer returned at the end of the day excited to see his new fence, but when he arrived he was shocked to see that the carpenter had not built a fence but a bridge. Soon after, his neighbor showed up and thanked the farmer for building such a beautifully crafted bridge and expressed his excitement that they were going to be friends again. The farmer acknowledged that the calf probably did belong to his neighbor, and the two were friends again.

Great negotiators are a bit like this carpenter. They are willing to be bold. They see opportunities others do not see. They are irrationally confident that a deal can happen or a problem can get solved. They are ambitious. But they are also empathetic: They see the deeper desire behind the initial ask. And they find ways to bring parties together. In this case, the carpenter saw an opportunity to restore a relationship and was courageous enough to chase it.

In your negotiations, you will have setbacks, surprises, and disappointments from the deals that don't get done, but each setback is also a learning opportunity. The tools provided in this book will enable you to see the bigger picture when you approach any negotiation so that you win the next deal, solve the next problem, maximize the next success, and overcome the people and circumstances that stand in the way of your dreams.

So what does life as a great negotiator look like? It means you will pursue a level of success that others will not. You will confidently tackle problems and challenges others will seek to avoid. As a great negotiator, you will become what others only hope to be. It means you will act boldly when others pause. You will also have opportunities to serve at levels that others will not. Great negotiators enjoy healthy relationships with family, friends, and colleagues. Finally, you will be able to make a difference in the arena while others watch from the stands.

There is a lot to gain from becoming a skilled negotiator. My goal with this book is to help you be more than just good at this skill: I want you to be great!

THE FIVE THINGS GREAT NEGOTIATORS KNOW

My knowledge of the negotiation process is the result of years of joining leaders in the trenches as they worked to put deals together and solve problems. I've identified five strategic skills that are fundamental to becoming a great negotiator. These skills enable negotiators to deliver outstanding results on a consistent basis.

While every negotiation comes with its own unexpected twists and turns, you don't want to come to the table unprepared. By learning the five fundamentals in this book, you will be able to manage the unexpected and also find the best path forward in any situation.

1. Great negotiators know how to manage themselves.

You don't have any control over how the other parties act or what they want in the negotiation process. But you do have control over yourself. That's why self-awareness is key. Set yourself up for success by knowing not every move will be easy or comfortable, checking your assumptions, making strategic decisions, mitigating your reactions, and moving forward with purpose.

2. Great negotiators know when to cooperate and when to compete.

The statement "He's a lover, not a fighter" reveals the two most common approaches to negotiation: cooperation (the lover) and competition (the fighter). People tend to approach problems using one of these two approaches. By the time you work through the book, you will know when it makes strategic sense to be a lover and when it is best to be a fighter to maximize your desired results.

3. Great negotiators know the most important move is the first move.

Once you select an approach, it's time to implement it. Great negotiators know how to make the critically important first move and the importance of managing expectations at the outset of a negotiation.

4. Great negotiators know how to solve problems using empathy and creativity.

Great negotiators can switch between cooperative and competitive approaches seamlessly. The cooperative approach uses empathy and creativity to understand the needs of the parties and generate possible solutions.

5. Great negotiators know how to satisfy all the parties.

At the end of the day, the purpose of negotiation is to deliver satisfaction. Once all parties are satisfied, you typically will have made your deal or solved your problem. Great negotiators know the elements of satisfaction and how to deliver it for all involved.

As you reflect on the five skills, you can score your current skill level through the Negotiation Made Simple Self-Assessment, found in the appendix. Don't judge yourself too harshly or overthink things; this is just to get a baseline.

Throughout this book we are going to explore these five fundamentals that great negotiators have mastered. You're going to learn how you can master them, too.

FINDING THE WHY IN NEGOTIATION

The author and inspirational speaker Simon Sinek masterfully challenged people and organizations to examine their "why" in his book *Start with Why*. He states that finding your why is a "process of discovery, not invention."[1] Therefore, before we take off down the road of exploring what to do and how to do it in negotiation, let's start with why. My why has two parts.

A few years ago, one of my graduate students handed me an envelope after class one day. In it was a piece of paper with the word "hope" serving as an acronym for the following phrase:

H = Help
O = Other
P = People
E = Excel

I thanked the student for her note. The beautiful acronym she shared helped me discover the first part of my why. It helped me conceptualize my why as a professional negotiator and consultant.

My why for writing this book is specifically to help other people excel in negotiation. It presents a simple, straightforward framework that you can use in any negotiation, no matter how difficult or complex. As you read on, you will get the tools needed to deliver outstanding negotiation outcomes and achieve your next success.

So what about you? What is your why? What can you accomplish by learning and using the strategies and skills offered in this book? What problems are you looking to solve through negotiation and how will it benefit your organization, career, or relationships if those problems are solved successfully?

To help you stay connected with your why, I invite you to identify a negotiation from your life that you can use as an application tool throughout the reading of this book. Perhaps it's the next deal you are working to land. Or maybe it is a problem of yours that desperately needs to be resolved. It can be a personal or a professional negotiation. Take a few moments to outline your negotiation on a notecard or piece of paper you can keep tucked inside this book, or go to negotiationmadesimple.com to fill out an online form that will capture the details of your negotiation. Consider the following questions:

- Who are the parties?
- What is the negotiation about?
- What do you want?

- What does the other side want?
- What are the potential barriers to getting a deal?

As you read this book, consider how each idea and tool can be applied to your negotiation to deliver the outcome that you desire. This roadmap will prove immediately useful as you manage this negotiation and countless others throughout your life. Let's get started on the journey toward your life as a great negotiator!

Part I
Manage Yourself

CHAPTER ONE

YOU ARE A NEGOTIATOR

> Everything is negotiable. Whether or not the negotiation is
> easy is another thing.
>
> —CARRIE FISHER[1]

When you hear the word *negotiation*, what comes to mind?

You might imagine people dressed in business attire, sitting across from one another at a table in a conference room. Maybe you're thinking about the last time you haggled with a car salesman. Perhaps you're remembering a squabble with your teenager over how late their curfew will be. Phrases like *bargain*, *give and take*, *win-win*, or *getting what I want* might come to mind.

All of these associations make sense, but consider this working definition: negotiation is a strategic communication process to make a deal or solve a problem.

By this definition, much of what we do in our day-to-day lives is really a negotiation. Think back to last week. Consider every meeting, every email, every interaction with customers or colleagues. What percentage of your time did you spend engaged in a strategic communication process to get a deal or resolve a problem? If you are a businessperson, you likely spend over half your time engaged in the negotiation process, but you may not realize it. Some of you spend almost 100 percent of your time negotiating! In fact, the English word *negotiation* is derived from the Latin root word *negotiatus*, which means to "carry on business." Negotiation is at the core of what you do to manage your employees and contractors, satisfy your customers, and grow your business or organization.

Negotiation, however, is not just a professional skill. Think of your personal life: Every day, you're arranging carpools, deciding what to cook for dinner, dating, making purchases, or disciplining a child. In each of these situations, are you communicating to make a deal or resolve a problem? Absolutely.

On the flip side, *not* thinking of ourselves as negotiators can have near-catastrophic results. In fact, we nearly had a nuclear war because of it!

THE DANGER OF NOT SEEING YOURSELF AS A NEGOTIATOR

One of my favorite movies involving negotiation is *Thirteen Days*. Based on the memoir by the late Robert Kennedy, it depicts the often-heated discussions among key advisers in the executive committee (or ExCom) advising President John F. Kennedy during the thirteen days of the Cuban Missile Crisis. In one scene, the Russian ships have violated the US blockade as they approach Cuba. The US Navy is deciding what to do in response, sparking a tense exchange between Admiral George Anderson and Robert McNamara, the US secretary of defense. The Navy admiral directs star shells to be fired over the Russian ship: star shells make noise and light, but they are not meant to cause significant damage.

Even so, McNamara sees this as a huge problem. He immediately lashes out at the admiral, concerned those star shells could be interpreted as an attack, starting the war everyone fears.

The Navy admiral tells McNamara to get out of his way and proudly states that the Navy has been running blockades since the time of John Paul Jones (the famous naval commander from the Revolutionary War). He doesn't need advice from McNamara.

In response to the proud admiral, McNamara yells, "You don't understand a thing, do you, Admiral?" He goes on to explain how the positioning of ships in the Caribbean Sea is the language President Kennedy and Secretary Nikita Khrushchev of the Communist Party of the Soviet Union are using to negotiate with each other. He describes it as a language the world has never seen. It's not war: it's *communication*.

The United States was seconds away from nuclear war because some of our leaders had no idea they were negotiating. This example is an extreme but effective one: if we do not always see ourselves as negotiators, we will make serious mistakes because we're not seeing the situation clearly.

One of the biggest mistakes we can make is thinking that negotiation is an incidental aspect of our job description— something we do occasionally or something that other people use, not us. We edit it out of our job title completely. We think of ourselves as professionals, as experts in our field, as leaders, managers, and partners. *But not negotiators.*

When we start treating negotiation like an occasional responsibility instead of a daily tool, we neglect it. We don't focus on it as much as other aspects of our job or our lives. We don't try to get better at it, and when it comes time to negotiate, we just wing it. And think of all the miscommunication, lost opportunities, and damage done simply because we don't approach situations with the right perspective. We give in when we should offer an alternative. We fight when we should cooperate. We miss out on a better outcome because we completely skip the step of strategic communication.

But if you start treating negotiation seriously, like a skill to practice and improve on, you will reap the benefits. Negotiation will make you a better leader, boss, employee, parent, spouse, and any other role you hold in life.

YOU NEGOTIATE CONSTANTLY IN YOUR DAILY LIFE

We've all had arguments with our parents, and I'm reminded of that when I'm raising my kids. Managing the naps, meals, car seats, play dates, and loss of sleep can be exhausting for parents. When my kids were younger, the nightly rhythm in the Lowry house went something like this:

My wife and kids would go to bed around 9:00 p.m. I would stay up a bit longer to prepare for the next day, watch TV, and eventually would go to bed around 11:00 p.m. At some point in the middle of the night, I would hear footsteps coming down the hall. Then the door to my bedroom would open. About this time, I would feel a nudge in my back from my wife. It was her way of telling me, "It's your turn!" Knowing what was best for me, I would jump out of bed, having just experienced my *first* negotiation of the day.

There, by the side of the bed, would be my son Deacon asking, "Can I sleep with you?" Agreeing to this request would guarantee a night full of restless sleep as Deacon would flail around between my wife and me for the remainder of the night. So I would object, "No buddy, let's go back to your bed and I'll put you to sleep." Notice that I am experiencing my *second* negotiation of the day with my son. Some nights, Deacon would comply. Other nights, he would begin to cry, insisting on sleeping with my wife and me. When he cried, he would wake up my other kids, often leading to my *third* and sometimes *fourth* negotiation of the day in working to get them back to sleep.

Those of you with young kids know what I am talking about. There are many nights when you will engage in one or more negotiations before you have to get up in the morning! Negotiation is not only the skill that gets us through the day; it is also the skill that gets parents through the night. And yet, most of us have done almost nothing to prepare for this process that will consume a majority of our time, determine our career success, and influence the relationships with the people we love. As a result, we have learned this important process through experience, success, and perhaps even a few hard knocks. As the following story demonstrates, just like the admiral in *Thirteen Days*, some of you may not even recognize that what you do is actually negotiation.

In recent years, I have conducted a negotiation training for the new class of engineers at the Tennessee Department of Transportation (TDOT). These young and talented professionals have been educated at some of the finest engineering schools in the southeastern United States, including Auburn, Georgia Tech, and Vanderbilt. These new engineers do not see themselves initially as negotiators—they are consumed by the technical aspects of their jobs and are still learning to see a larger picture.

In a recent class, one of the engineers declared that he *never* negotiates as part of his work for TDOT and did not think negotiation was relevant to his success. I asked him to describe the most significant project he was working on at that moment. The engineer discussed an incident analysis he was asked to prepare for a particular road in rural Tennessee. I inquired about its purpose, and he mentioned local demand for TDOT to conduct this analysis because of a perceived high number of accidents at this turn in the road. I then asked him what the local elected officials wanted from TDOT, and he mentioned the demand from local officials for TDOT to redesign this turn to make it safer for motorists. At this point in the conversation, the young engineer smiled and shook his head as he realized his entire assignment was a negotiation between public officials on how to most effectively and efficiently reduce the number of accidents at that turn in the road.

Upon realizing the importance of negotiation to their success, these engineers acknowledged the technical aspects of their formal education were not enough. Learning to negotiate was not a major part of the engineering curriculum at their institution of higher learning. Yet it would be the skill that defined a great deal of their success as an engineer and eventually as a manager or leader of engineers.

BECOME A PROFESSIONAL NEGOTIATOR

Do me a favor: Take a minute to find one of your business cards. Take note of your title. Perhaps you are a president or vice president or maybe an owner or associate. Some of us are specialists or managers. Many of our titles have to do with our profession: attorney, accountant, pastor, counselor.

Notice that your title clearly describes your position. It gives people a sense of your level in your company or organization, and it may even suggest your profession. But it does *not* accurately describe what you do to be successful. To be successful, you manage a strategic communication process to make deals or solve problems. In other words, to be successful, you negotiate. You're not paid to wear a certain name tag. You're paid to negotiate.

The starting point is to see ourselves as negotiators.

Stop thinking of yourself as a job title who negotiates, and start seeing yourself as a negotiator who achieves results.

Negotiation is sometimes painted as a boring subject: something for the suits in the boardroom. After reading this book, I want you to realize that negotiation is exciting by nature. You can never be absolutely sure what's going to happen in a negotiation, and the stakes are often high. My hope is to prepare you for the unusual or unexpected events that can arise in this process to help you succeed.

Think about the game show *Deal or No Deal*. It's a forty-two-minute negotiation between the contestant and the banker in a studio in Hollywood. *Shark Tank* is a seven-minute negotiation between the entrepreneurs and the sharks. Movies like *The Negotiator* with Samuel L. Jackson depict high-stakes, sometimes life-or-death, negotiations.

By investing in your negotiation skills, you're getting ahead. Less than 10 percent of professionals have ever received formal training or taken a course to develop their negotiation skills. By reading this book and completing the exercises, you will be in the 10 percent of people who are negotiating based off a strategic framework, as opposed to just winging it based on experience or hard knocks.

You can start using these tactics and experiencing success right away.

Take a pen and scratch out the title on your business card and in the space where your title used to be write, "Professional Negotiator." That is your new title. Use that business card as your bookmark as you read this book to remind yourself over and over again of your new title. Once you begin to see yourself as a negotiator and see what you do as negotiation, you will be in a better position to apply what you learn to generate your next level of success.

Build Your Framework—How to Embrace Your Role as a Professional Negotiator

- Know your success depends on how well you negotiate.
- Develop a deep understanding of the negotiation process.
- Commit to mastering negotiation skills.
- Be intentional about leveraging your knowledge and skill into great negotiation outcomes.

Think It Through

- What do you negotiate in your professional life?
- What do you negotiate in your personal life?

For more negotiation tools and content,
please visit negotiationmadesimple.com.

CHAPTER TWO

STRATEGY WINS

The essence of strategy is choosing what not to do.

—MICHAEL PORTER,
Harvard Business School[1]

Do me a favor and fold your arms. Now, take the arm that is on the bottom and put it on top. Can you do it? How does it feel? It's awkward and uncomfortable, right? Absolutely!

When I asked you to fold your arms, did you work through a cognitive thought process to determine whether to put your right arm or left arm on top? Probably not. You just folded your arms like you always fold your arms and did it the way that is comfortable for you.

Feeling natural or comfortable drives much of our behavior, guiding our decisions and actions. It governs the situations we put ourselves in and dictates many of our choices as consumers. We are constantly working to make ourselves feel comfortable. Ironically, as I write these words, I am sitting up in bed with the covers over me because it is cold, and I want to be comfortable.

This relentless pursuit of comfort also informs how we negotiate. We don't like to do things that don't make sense or are uncomfortable. *Negotiation is a process we cannot master unless we are willing to do hard things that are uncomfortable.* Mastering the negotiation process will require us to ask for things the other side doesn't want to give. It will compel us to say no to demands. It will create conflict as we pursue our interests and desires. All of these things are uncomfortable, but at times they are necessary to be successful.

Let's go back to the folding arms exercise. The fact is, we are capable of folding our arms in a different way. It's just harder and feels awkward. It will be this way until we master the new technique. As a negotiator, you must go beyond what is comfortable and begin doing what is strategic. This means using your targeted outcome and ultimate objective as the driving force behind every decision and move you make in a negotiation. Acting strategically will not always be comfortable and will likely require us to do hard things.

DO HARD THINGS

Great negotiators do the hard things to get results. They become so skilled at negotiating that even though they are uncomfortable, they can successfully carry out their strategy without showing their discomfort. This is the mountaintop of managing yourself as a negotiator.

The first hard thing you will need to do is develop your knowledge of the negotiation process. As you develop knowledge about this process, you will acquire and practice more skills. Growing your skills will make you more confident in managing the difficult moments of negotiation. As you become more confident, you will be better able to act in a strategic manner that leads to great success.

Knowledge   Skill   Confidence   Comfort   Success

My friend Don Miller showed me a Bell's Whisky commercial several years ago.[2] It chronicled the story of an elderly man's journey of learning to read. He sat in class sounding out words with his teacher and went to the children's section of the library to find books he could read. Eventually, he transitioned to reading adult books and began staying up late at night to read a specific book in his home. The man finally walked into a bar with that book in his hand. He walked up to a man at the bar and said, "Son, I read your book."

The emotion of the moment is overwhelming as you reflect back on this man's journey to learn to read just so he could celebrate his son's success in writing a book. This dad did the hard thing so he could generate the right result with his son. It is a powerful lesson for us as negotiators. This process requires us to do hard things that are at times uncomfortable to get the right result!

DECISIONS MUST BE MADE IN THE FACE OF UNCERTAINTY

Once you have developed the courage to go beyond what is comfortable, you must learn to deal with the uncertainty that clouds this entire process. In negotiation, it's rarely the case that "all the cards" are on the table. *Negotiation requires you to make decisions in the face of great uncertainty.* How many times do you have all the information you would like when putting a deal together? Almost never. You rarely know the bottom line of the other side. They may share information with you, but the information might not be complete or 100 percent accurate.

Uncertainty comes in many forms. It doesn't just exist because of a lack of information. It exists because the elements of deception are often present in the negotiation process. When your teenager asks you to stay out late, they are often vague about who they are with or what they are up to. If a client tells you that you have full creative control of a project, what they aren't telling you is that they have already looped several people into the project. A contractor will promise something they don't have the authority to guarantee.

Deception is the act of suggesting people believe something that is not true.[3] This is a form of influence that is an appropriate and accepted part of the negotiation process. For example, a seller might say in a business transaction, "I cannot let this product go for one penny less than $25,000. That's my best deal." Despite taking this position and making this clear statement, the seller wants to get the deal, so he agrees to a final concession that gets the deal at $24,500. Is the seller a liar? Perhaps technically, but this kind of thing happens in negotiation all the time. The seller is not considered to be behaving unethically because some level of deception is an accepted part of this process, and it is the presence of deception that creates uncertainty in negotiation.

Before I leave the topic of deception, it is important to note two important ethical considerations for negotiators. First, you cannot commit fraud. Fraud is knowingly misrepresenting a material fact that is relied upon to the detriment of another. In the example above, is the seller committing fraud by saying he will not sell a product for less than $25,000? No, because it is not a material fact. But one must be careful not to deceive others as to the nature of the product. If the seller knowingly represents that the product is an upgraded version when it is in fact a standard version, then they have committed fraud. Negotiators must be careful to not knowingly misrepresent material facts in the negotiation process.

Second, negotiators do not have to lie to be successful. I know many negotiators who, to preserve their credibility, will not make any statements to influence the other side that are not 100 percent accurate. While a little exaggeration or "spin" is to be expected, lying is not the path to successful negotiation outcomes. How you conduct yourself within the negotiation process is an important strategic decision. But whether you decide to engage in deception or not, you must anticipate that others will use it as a tool for getting ahead in the negotiation process, which will force you to make decisions in the face of uncertainty.

DON'T LET YOUR INTUITION LEAD YOU ASTRAY

When we are faced with uncertainty and not prepared for it, we end up guessing how to respond. We use our intuition—which might seem reliable—but really we're reaching for whatever feels most comfortable and logical to us. That intuitive reaction will be different for everyone, but *your intuition can actually lead you astray in negotiation.*

For some, being caught off guard with uncertainty prompts them to become very trusting. We tend to rely on others for information and don't question it. For others, intuition leads them to become competitive and hold their cards close to the vest. Either way, people make assumptions and run with them.

When faced with uncertainty, most of us lean into our intuition and hope that it will work out. Rather than trusting your intuition, *managing yourself in the midst of uncertainty means having a framework that you follow with discipline.*

Let me give you an example of how easily intuition can lead us astray. Years ago, a client of mine was negotiating a commercial real estate lease. He was friends with the owner of the building. When his company wanted to lease some space, he assumed his friend would treat him fairly and give him a good deal. His friend made several promises about things he would do to improve the building. My client took his word for it and never thought for a minute he wouldn't come through, signing the lease trusting in his friend's promises. A few weeks after my client signed the lease, a letter came from a company he had not heard of. It stated that it had purchased the building and gave an address where to send the rent. My client inquired with both the new owner and his "friend" (the old owner) about all the promised improvements. To this day, none have been completed.

My client's intuition to trust his friend was based on a faulty (and unconscious) assumption: that his friend valued the relationship as much as he did. My client ended up putting too much stock in the relationship and paid for it. He assumed that he had all the information. But he didn't. He should have utilized former president Ronald Reagan's famous "trust, but verify" approach. He didn't and his assumptions ended up causing him to lose something of substantial value.

THE ONLY THING YOU CAN CONTROL

When there's a lot of uncertainty at play, the only thing you can do is control your actions. You can't control what other people are keeping from you, what they want out of the situation, or how they react to you. You can manage only yourself.

That means questioning yourself and your assumptions. To me, the lesson in my client's real estate mistake is not that he should never trust anyone or that it's never a good idea to go into business with one's friends. Nor do I think he has bad intuition. How could he have known that his friend would act that way? He couldn't have known. He didn't have all the information. That is the moral of the story.

Even when you *think* you have all the information, you probably don't. This is why it's so important to manage yourself.

What my friend failed to do was examine himself in the beginning and bring to light his own assumptions: namely, that his friend would not let him down. And because he wasn't aware of that assumption, he just moved along without questioning it. You may say this outcome was the result of an unethical or deceptive business practice. But I see a problem much closer to home: My friend did not examine his instincts going into the negotiation. He made faulty assumptions. He was comfortable, so he acted and left himself vulnerable to being exploited in the negotiation. Basically, he did not manage himself well at all.

Uncertainty will always be present in negotiation. We can't know what we don't know. But it's precisely for that reason that we need to know how to manage ourselves in the face of uncertainty.

Do you want to know one thing you can always know? *Yourself.*

"Know thyself" is advice introduced by the ancient philosophers and affirmed by many of today's self-help gurus. *Self-awareness is the first step toward becoming a great negotiator.* Some people have so much personality that it literally fills up the entire room. Others are wallflowers and would rather read a book than talk to anyone. Negotiation by its very nature involves interaction between two or more individuals— who each have unique personality traits that can mix like oil and water or like the ideal pairing of peanut butter and jelly.

Given that negotiation is often driven by relationship building, introverts can find themselves at a disadvantage. Not only may they not be more comfortable keeping their cards close to the vest, they may also hurt themselves by keeping quiet about key information.

In contrast, as one researcher noted, those who are extroverts tend to come alive in negotiations as they prefer working in group settings and can feel and respond to emotional displays more effectively. Introverts, on the other hand, can find socializing uncomfortable and even negative.[4]

That said, it actually doesn't take much for introverts to succeed in interacting with others in negotiations. Researchers from Northwestern University explored how introverts can overcome personality deficits and found that you don't have to go very far out of your comfort zone to make a connection with your counterpart.[5] In one study, those who engaged in a short, five-minute phone call beforehand were four times more likely to reach a good agreement than those who didn't have a call.[6]

Introverts would be well served to consider whether a bit of friendly banter before negotiations, however uncomfortable, might be beneficial for the final outcome and even practice negotiation sessions to gain confidence when the time comes. An array of researchers and academics have also noted that being an introvert can be a strength in negotiating, as introverts more often ask for and consider others' opinions than extroverts do and are typically more deliberative and less impulsive in their decision-making approach.[7]

I am impressed with this very practical idea that flows from the research. I use it often in my practice and find it to be wildly effective. One of the simplest ways to increase camaraderie and personal bonding that is proven to help achieve successful outcomes in the negotiation is sharing a cup of coffee or a meal together. Ayelet Fishbach, a professor at the University of Chicago Booth School of Business, argues that when people share not only a meal but actually share a plate, they often collaborate better and reach deals faster.[8]

"Basically, every meal that you're eating alone is a missed opportunity to connect to someone," she says. "And every meal that involves food sharing fully utilizes the opportunity to create that social bond."[9]

Fishbach notes that sharing meals is customary in Chinese and Indian cultures. In her experiment, one group was given a bowl of chips and salsa to share, while another was given their own individual portions, and then each were given a negotiation scenario. The group with shared bowls struck agreement faster and at significant savings.[10]

Whether an introvert or an extrovert, you should also have a sense of your instinct and assumptions in the face of uncertainty. Some people are naturally more trusting and willing to be cooperative. Others look out for themselves and tend to be more guarded and competitive in the face of uncertainty. Both approaches can be good, but both can also get you into trouble.

For instance, our unconscious desire to do what is comfortable or to avoid tension can lead to us making decisions and offers that ultimately do not serve us well in the negotiation process. These things are ways we justify losing. Alternatively, our tendency to come in with fists swinging can also ruin a deal or a relationship before negotiations even begin.

For my friend, the commercial real estate example was a hard lesson to learn about tendencies and assumptions. It is natural to want to be cooperative with friends and business associates we know well. But self-awareness reminds us to check ourselves before negotiating. It's not that you should never trust or be cooperative: it's that you make sure your trust is well placed and your approach doesn't leave you open to being exploited.

Assumptions aren't just about whom we trust. When it comes to negotiating, we can make lots of assumptions: how the process will work, who will speak first, what the other people want, what's best for ourselves or the other party, or what moves the other person will make. There is so much room for error.

The best way to combat these assumptions is to know our default, check them with reality, and manage our own expectations. You can do this with the following framework to help you assess and manage yourself.

FOUR QUESTIONS FOR MANAGING YOURSELF

Take a minute to think about a situation you're facing right now in which you're negotiating a solution to a problem. Ask yourself the following four questions and challenge yourself to answer them honestly.

These are helpful questions to ask at any stage of a negotiation but especially in the beginning stages as parties are taking their positions. There will always be unknown factors. But self-awareness empowers us to make a different choice.

1. **What assumptions am I making to fill in the information I do not have?** This question prompts you to list the information you do and do not have. It brings uncertainty to light, and then it asks you to name any assumptions that you're making.

2. **What is the basis for these assumptions, and is that basis legitimate?** This question prompts you to check in with reality. Not all assumptions are unfounded, but all are worth questioning.

3. **Are your assumptions based on what you *hope* to be the case or what is actually the case?** There is a famous business book entitled *Hope Is Not a Strategy*.[11] It reminds business leaders that hoping for the best is probably not a sound strategy for preparing to launch a new business or growing revenues in the coming year. The same is true here. As much as we want to hope for the best, we must deal with reality. What are the facts, good or bad? What are reasonable assumptions, positive or negative? What should you expect from the other side, helpful or difficult? Keep it real with your assumptions.

4. **What information am I using to build a strategy, and can I rely on that information to be accurate?** Identify the key pieces of information that you are using to make strategic decisions and consider whether there is a chance that information may not be reliable. Is the information consistent with other facts or past experiences leading up to the negotiation? I have plaintiffs' attorneys tell me all the time they are ready and eager to take a case to trial. They follow up by telling me how big the verdict will be and how my client will be left with a public relations disaster following a potential eye-popping

verdict. In some cases, however, I find the plaintiff's attorney really doesn't like to try cases and has trouble winning at trial. These facts undermine the information being shared with me in the midst of the negotiation, information that is useful for making strategic decisions that are in the best interest of my client.

OVERCOMING THE UNCERTAINTY

Let's now return to the original example. Say that, instead of my client trusting his friend implicitly, he had stopped to ask these questions. He might have realized there was a chance his friend's promises would not materialize. After all, it was not in his financial interest to complete all these improvements at his expense. For this reason, my client might have insisted that these promises be included in writing in the contract, which would have given him legal recourse if they were not fulfilled. He might have asked that the improvements be completed before occupying the space. He might have negotiated a better outcome.

Our path to overcoming uncertainty is to have as much self-awareness as possible. If we do not examine our decisions against a good strategy, we are left with making decisions based on assumptions. When we're not aware of how we react to uncertainty, we unconsciously let our instincts rule the negotiation, and this does not always work out well for us.

My challenge to you is to understand the dynamics of how you think and behave as a negotiator. This self-knowledge will be the groundwork for a disciplined framework for making decisions and managing moves.

You will find yourself losing less often and winning much more of the time.

Build Your Framework—How to Negotiate in the Midst of Uncertainty

- Recognize that uncertainty will be part of every negotiation.
- Become self-aware of your personal tendencies in the face of uncertainty.
- Determine how much you resist doing hard things that are uncomfortable in negotiation. If you can't do it, engage someone who can on your behalf.
- Test your assumptions. Are they based in reality, or do you hope something to be true that really isn't?
- Reflect on whether your trust of the other side is rational. Are they incentivized to cooperate or compete with you?
- Move slowly and carefully until you have enough information and experience negotiating with the other side to reduce the uncertainty.

Think It Through

- What part of "you" must you manage carefully in a negotiation?
- Reflect on a time when someone took advantage of your trust. What assumptions did you make that allowed this to happen? How can you avoid such situations going forward?

For more negotiation tools and content,
please visit negotiationmadesimple.com.

CHAPTER THREE

SUCCESS STARTS WITH YOU

It starts with you.

—DWAYNE "THE ROCK" JOHNSON[1]

Imagine you are getting ready to sell your house. It's a smaller, one-story house in a decent neighborhood. You have cleaned out all of the clutter and are in the process of staging the home in a way that will get you top dollar. You have surveyed the market and believe $600,000 would be a good asking price for the house.

One day, as you are cleaning out your house, your neighbors approach you in the yard. They are a retired couple who live across the street in a big, two-story house and always seem to have grandchildren running around. They mention to you that they have noticed all the trucks in the driveway and the furniture coming in and out, and they ask you if you are getting ready to sell it. You tell them you haven't listed it with a real estate agent yet but are ready to sell.

What they say next surprises you. They talk about their need for a one-story home and how they will do anything to stay in the neighborhood because their grandchildren live down the street. They have been looking for a one-story house in the neighborhood for years but haven't had any luck. Next, they talk about how your house would be perfect for them as they are looking to downsize and age in place.

They then ask you the big question: "How much are you going to ask for your house?"

What is your answer?

My guess is some of you would say $650,000 or maybe even $700,000. The retired couple just admitted they're "willing to do anything" to stay in the neighborhood, and you also want to be prepared in case they counteroffer. At the end of the day, you may get more for your home and your neighbors would have an ideal location to live out their retirement. Why not pursue that deal?

Others would immediately say $600,000, since that is, in fact, the price that you have in mind. Why try to exploit your elderly neighbors? You have a bird in hand. Take the deal! Some may even say $575,000 knowing that you will save on the realtor commissions. After all, they are your longtime neighbors.

Do you hear the multiple voices in your head suggesting different answers? You have a mix of various motives. You want to help them, but you also want to help yourself. You want to close the deal, but you don't want to settle for less than what you could get in the marketplace.

COMPETITIVE VOICES IN YOUR HEAD

- "I want to win."
- "Let's claim all the value we can get."
- "Ask for more and you will get more."
- "I want the best deal possible no matter what."

COOPERATIVE VOICES IN YOUR HEAD

- "I want to get a deal."
- "Let's work with them to create value that benefits us all."
- "You have to give to get."
- "You catch more flies with honey."

This is the negotiator's dilemma. How competitive or cooperative should you be to get the best deal? What strategy should you use to approach this negotiation? Should you claim value from the other side or create it with the other side?

THE LOVER VERSUS THE FIGHTER: TWO STRATEGIES FOR NEGOTIATION

You've heard that famous saying, "He's a lover, not a fighter."

Generally, there are two main approaches to negotiation: a cooperative one and a competitive. I have compared them to the general archetypes of "lover" and "fighter."

The "lover" represents the cooperative approach. With this approach, you see the solution as something that would be both beneficial and satisfying for both parties. You try to help the other side get what they want while at the same time pursuing what you want. You look to work together and create value for everyone involved. This approach is marked by accommodation and collaboration, trying to create value by working toward a solution that satisfies everyone.

A competitive approach sees the negotiation as a fight for value: there's a winner and a loser. With this approach, you are more ambitious and want to claim value. You tend to protect yourself and are not as trusting of others. You're looking to set yourself up to win as much as possible even if it means the other side will lose. This approach is marked by big asks and hard bargains.

As you'll find out, you have a natural tendency for one or the other. Your personality, cultural background, societal influences, observations of negotiation, and experience all come together to shape your natural style or approach. But it's important to not just lean on an approach that is natural or comfortable. There are times, for example, when it's devastating to *both* parties for one to lean on the cooperative approach. Other times, being too competitive can kill any chance of a deal before a negotiation even starts. *A great negotiator knows how to use both of these approaches and employ them at different moments in a negotiation to get the best result.* Let's lay it out for you visually (see figure 1).

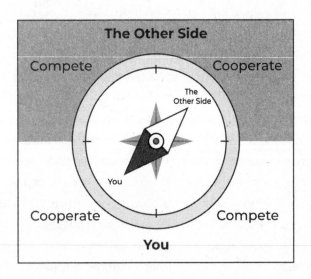

FIGURE 1

So how do we learn how to evaluate a negotiation and employ the correct strategy? I'll walk you through it step-by-step.

CHOOSING TO COMPETE OR COOPERATE: SIX FOUNDATIONAL THINGS YOU SHOULD KNOW

Before you decide which path to go down, there are a few negotiation dynamics you should know about:

Know the game you are playing.

It is essential to know if you are negotiating with someone who is competitive or someone who is cooperative. Their approach should influence yours. Of course, knowing what approach they are taking is not as simple as just asking them. Imagine sitting down at the table to negotiate the purchase of a business. You begin by asking the owners if they are looking to capture all the value in the deal or if they are open to sharing the value so you could get a win yourself. It would be an awkward start to the negotiation, and it is unlikely that they would be that transparent with their strategy. So how do you know the other side's approach? By observing the nature of the moves and understanding the meaning behind them. It's not what the other side *says*, it's what they *do* in the negotiation that loudly declares how they are approaching the deal.

When I was practicing law, I recall being assigned to a new case. The opposing counsel was an experienced and well-respected lawyer. A few weeks after the case had been filed, I received a letter from opposing counsel. It was unlike any other letter I had ever received from an opposing attorney. The letter went something like this:

Dear Mr. Lowry:

As you know, I represent plaintiff A. Smith in *Smith v. ABC Hospital* in the Case No. 01-23-45678 in the First Judicial District Court of Davidson County, Texas, in which you are the attorney of record representing ABC Hospital. I look forward to working with you to reach a timely and amicable resolution of this matter. To that end, I hope you will join me in entering a Rule 11 agreement pertaining to our professionalism and conduct as attorneys in this case.

   This will confirm that you have agreed to conduct yourself throughout the course of this litigation with the utmost professional courtesy and respect. You have agreed to maintain the highest level of ethical conduct on behalf of your client and before the court. You have agreed to fully, accurately, and timely respond to discovery requests in compliance with the Texas Rules of Evidence and Texas Rules of Civil Procedure. Finally, you have agreed to be reasonable with respect to scheduling, communications, settlement negotiations, and issues that arise during the course of this litigation.

   Thank you in advance for your agreement pertaining to our professional conduct in this matter.

Very truly yours,
John Doe

When I first received the letter I went down the hall to ask a colleague for his advice on how to respond. He said emphatically, "*Don't sign that letter.*" He then went on to explain how the attorney would pull that letter out or send a copy every time I did something in the course of the case that he didn't like. I learned the letter was not a step toward peace; it was in fact a weapon. The opposing attorney didn't use the letter to create an amicable approach to resolving the case but instead used it as a way to try to control my behavior and decisions related to the case. The attorney's behavior would be outrageously aggressive, but he would try to hold me to my commitments in the letter.

If I had not asked for advice from a colleague, I would have likely signed the letter based on what it said. But what it said was not important. It was the behavior and positioning of the opposing counsel that were more accurate indicators of whether I was in a cooperative or competitive negotiation. Despite the suggestion of the words in the letter, I was actually in a highly competitive negotiation with this attorney and needed to proceed accordingly.

Each move has substance and a signal.

The best negotiators recognize each move in the process has both substance and a signal. The substance is what is exchanged with each move. This may be money, time, discounts, services, or units. The signal is the "tell." What is the person saying to you about how they are approaching the deal by the moves being made? What do these moves symbolize? By evaluating the signal in the move, you can pick up on the nature of the game you are playing. An outrageous opening offer usually suggests it will be a competitive negotiation. A reasonable offer with an inquiry as to what you are looking to achieve in the negotiation might suggest it will be a more cooperative process.

You can't cooperate in the midst of competition.

As evidenced by my friend's real estate lease mistake I told you about earlier, people primarily lose in a negotiation because they take a cooperative approach in response to a competitive negotiation. Some people employ a cooperative approach when they really should compete because they misinterpret the nature of the negotiation. They make assumptions not based in reality. Others use the cooperative approach because it feels right. It's more comfortable than a competitive approach.

But the truth is that competition chokes out cooperation. If the other side is committed to a competitive approach, and you aren't willing to match the competition, you'll lose 100 percent of the time. So how do we know when it's time to get competitive? When someone takes an extreme position, they display one of a few signals that they are taking a competitive approach. An unreasonable start forces a competitive negotiation. We must match their move—or as some may call it retaliate—to ensure that we don't get exploited.

It sometimes takes competition to produce cooperation.

One of the ironic truths of mixed motives is that sometimes competition is required to bring about cooperation. Think about it: If the competitive party is able to extract the concessions they want from the cooperative party they're negotiating with, why should they ever change strategies? What they are doing is getting them what they want.

But when we counter the extreme positions of our opponents with extreme positions of our own, we create distance between the parties. This distance suggests that a deal might not happen. Likely, not being able to reach a deal is a loss for both parties. This forces each to be a little more cooperative. If they want to come to an agreement, they have to start considering what the other party wants. They have to change their strategy. But sometimes to get to that point of cooperation, you have to first use competition.

There is a cost to competition.

Just because competition sometimes leads to cooperation doesn't mean it's always the perfect solution. Sophisticated negotiators also recognize there is a cost to competition. Being too competitive at the wrong time in the negotiation can break down trust, and instead of leading to cooperation, it actually shuts down the negotiation. You will miss opportunities to create benefits for both parties because the trust isn't there—and, in extreme cases, the deal actually might not happen at all. As a negotiator, you must be careful not to win the battle but lose the war.

The best deals go to those who know when to compete and when to cooperate.

Do competitive negotiators get good deals? The answer is yes. Competitive negotiators get good deals because they are ambitious, they don't take unnecessary risks, and they usually ask for more. Do cooperative negotiators get good deals? The answer is yes again. Cooperative negotiators get good deals because they can generate trust, get people to give, and create a spirit of mutual benefit around the negotiation.

So, who gets the best deals? The answer is *the negotiators who know when to be competitive and when to be cooperative and are skilled in carrying out both strategies.* While you can't employ both methods at the same time, you can switch between them. You must be prepared to use both. That's how to get the best deal, every time.

The question is, how do you decide which is the appropriate approach for the situation?

HOW TO DECIDE YOUR APPROACH TO A NEGOTIATION

I believe pilots and negotiators have a lot in common. The decisions they make are consequential. There is much they can control, but there is a lot they do not control. Things can go wrong quickly, and they must be able to react and recover. Finally, they must decide on an approach.

The pilot must decide on an approach to a runway. This decision involves many factors, such as winds, visibility, air traffic, terrain, and so on. Systems and criteria are in place at each airport for determining whether to start an approach or not, and weather conditions will often dictate which type of approach a pilot will use. Even if the flight originated halfway around the world, the pilot must carefully and intentionally plan for the last half hour of the flight for it to end safely and successfully.

This is also true for negotiators. Planning your approach to the negotiation, taking into account relevant factors is critical to success. Here, you will learn how to strategically approach a negotiation.

Figure 2 is a modified version of one created by Ken Thomas and Ralph Kilmann. Years ago, they took their grid and created the Thomas-Kilmann Conflict Mode Instrument, one of the most popular inventories to measure a person's behavior in conflict situations. This grid is helpful for anyone today looking to determine which negotiation approach to take.[2]

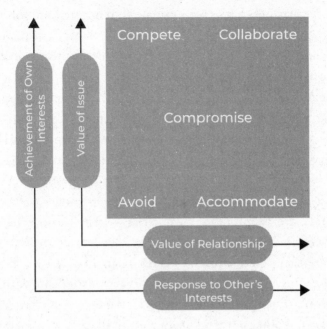

FIGURE 2

The process relies on your ability to evaluate how important an issue is to you and how important a relationship is to you. If the issue holds a lot of weight, you will rank it high on the y-axis, for competitive. If the relationship holds a lot of weight, you will rank it high on the x-axis, for cooperative. If the relationship is only kind of important to you, or the issue would only affect you a little bit, then you would graph it appropriately. At this point, you're weighing how important it is for you to get everything you want and considering if there's anything you would sacrifice. You're asking yourself if there's any way you can help the other party and evaluating if you'd want to do that (or what could incentivize you to do so). Here, the justice of your situation is what's most important, or whether you're willing to extend mercy to the other party.

Let's presume that as you evaluate your negotiation, you realize the issue is incredibly important to you (more so than the relationship), and that it's important to you to seek justice. Getting what is "right" is nonnegotiable. In this case, you're probably going to lean more on the side of the competitive approach. The more the issue or the details of the outcome mean to you, the less willing you would be to compromise. Here you would rank a negotiation high on the competitive axis.

On the other hand, if you're negotiating with someone who holds an important position in your life (a spouse, say), you would care deeply about what they want. Despite feeling wronged in some way, you would be motivated to have mercy toward them. In this case, it makes much more sense to adopt a cooperative approach. The value of the relationship with the other party, your willingness to extend mercy, and your desire to give the other party what they want all drive a cooperative approach. These values prompt you to try to create value for both sides and work together. Here you would rank an issue high on the x-axis for imperative.

The weight of each of these values (issue and relationship) lands you somewhere on the grid on page 35.

To illustrate each negotiation approach, let's use the scenario of someone at your front door.

THE FRONT DOOR NEGOTIATION IN FIVE SCENARIOS

1. Avoidance

You hear a knock on your door. When you answer, you find it's a neighbor who you don't know but who lives close by. They're complaining to you about the speed of traffic on the street.

They proceed to tell you they plan on making an appearance at the next city council meeting, and they're going to ask the city to take action to slow the traffic on the street: either through installing signage or speed bumps. Your neighbor invites you to be part of the collection of neighbors attending the city council meeting to champion this cause.

The truth is, you don't care about this issue. You don't think the traffic is too fast. In fact, you might be the one driving too fast down the street. In addition, you don't know this neighbor very well. You don't have a relationship or socialize with them.

Look at the graph: when the issue (a competitive approach value) is low and the relationship (a cooperative approach value) is low, the strategic move is to avoid engagement. You don't want to get caught up fighting for or against the issue because it doesn't matter to you. It also isn't important to you to appease your neighbor, since that relationship doesn't hold a lot of weight for you.

Here's what I want you to appreciate: most people avoid uncomfortable and difficult moments not because it's strategic but because they don't want to deal with the discomfort. Here, though, is a moment where it is strategic to avoid conflict, to save time and energy, and not get caught up in what doesn't matter to you.

2. Accommodation

You get a second knock on your door. It's one of your colleagues, standing there with her eight-year-old daughter. The girl hands you a clipboard and talks about how she's raising money for her school fundraiser. She's offering you an opportunity to buy a magazine.

If you strategically think about it, your colleague has really put you in a pickle because she knows the relationship is critically important. She also knows that you don't need or want a magazine. But the magazine doesn't cost that much. So the issue isn't that important (competitive), but the relationship (cooperative) is.

Likely, you will accommodate: buy a new subscription in order to keep a good relationship at work.

3. Competition

For sake of illustration, let's imagine something that hopefully never happens: You go to your door to find a person who threatens harm to you or your family. You're going to do whatever you need to protect yourself and your family.

In that particular moment, there is going to be no accommodation or avoidance. The issue of protecting your family is clearly very important. The relationship with the intruder is not important at all. Strategically, this is a moment where you're going to compete by whatever means necessary to protect those you love.

4. Compromise

What do you do when both the issue and the relationship are important to you?

Let's say the knock on the door is a mom down the street who often takes your kids to school. You switch off on carpool days, allowing you to get into the office early a few mornings of the week. She wants to add another neighbor into the carpool rotation. She tells you the teenager from the house down the street has offered to drive the kids on Mondays and Fridays. She tells you what a relief it would be for her not to drive those days. This relationship is important to you: You see your neighbor frequently, and your kids are friends. But you know the teenager she's talking about is not very responsible, and you're not about to let your kids get in the car with him. Unfortunately, you also have a staff meeting early on Monday mornings, and short of getting a sitter, you're not sure who else would easily drive the kids.

You tell her how much you appreciate her and explain that you just don't feel comfortable with a teen driving your kids. You offer to take the additional slot on Fridays if she'll still drive on Monday mornings.

In those moments, you're going to have to find a place of compromise. Compromise is not just a win-win. To compromise, you have to be able to give something up, and the other side has to be willing to give something up, too. This will require talking through the options and seeing what's agreeable to both sides.

5. Collaboration

When you're not willing to compromise on anything—when the relationship is extremely important and the issue is extremely important—then you will have to collaborate. To honor the relationship and protect the issue, you have to invite the other side to join you in collaboration to work on creative solutions.

Let's take a similar dilemma but change the circumstances: Let's say you cannot offer to take carpool duty on Friday because you have another mandatory meeting. Let's also say the person you're sharing carpool responsibilities with is not your neighbor but your partner. Your partner wants to utilize the teen down the street, and you don't feel comfortable with it, but you're not able to drive instead. The issues (both your work attendance and your kids' safety) are important but certainly you don't want to alienate your partner. This is when you need to collaborate. Together, you can brainstorm ways to free up both of your mornings while still getting the kids to school in a safe way.

Instead of simply being comfortable or doing what you're used to, be strategic. As you evaluate the importance of the issue and the importance of the relationship, use this grid to help you choose an approach that will honor what's important to you and lead you to the best possible outcome.

FIRST THINGS FIRST

Before I teach you how to win using competitive negotiation or how to achieve mutual gain using cooperative negotiation, it is important to first learn how not to lose. Your first objective is knowing how to avoid exploitation. We all have those stories in which we know we got taken to the cleaners or left money on the table. How do these stories make you feel? Horrible, right? I hate thinking about those moments in my negotiating past. Let's think about how to make sure that never happens again. What follows is an easy-to-remember four-step process for avoiding exploitation when you don't know when to compete or cooperate.

David Lax and James Sebenius in their classic book *The Manager as Negotiator* describe a process I'll call Axelrod's Four Steps, after the professor Robert Axelrod.[3] These steps will help you manage the tension between wanting to compete and wanting to cooperate. This is the process to use when you want to move from just doing what seems comfortable to a formulaic, strategic process.

Axelrod's Four Steps

Axelrod ran a computer game experiment, much like a computer chess tournament, based on the famous "Prisoner's

Dilemma" game from the Rand Institute in the 1950s.[4] As Axelrod describes the game, "[T]wo prisoners face the choice of informing on each other or remaining silent . . . [and] each must make the choice without knowing what the other will do."[5] After conducting his experiment, Axelrod made four observations that he formulated into what is often a very successful negotiating strategy.[6]

1. **Start cooperatively.** The cooperative approach to a deal— or the "nice" strategy as Axelrod calls it—is an easier, more preferable process.[7] Therefore, give it a chance. This is why Axelrod's approach says to start cooperatively.[8] Test whether the other side is willing to cooperate. If they are, you might have an easy path to a deal.

2. **Respond in kind.** After the other side makes their move, evaluate the signal. Is it a competitive or cooperative move? If its competitive, then retaliate. If its cooperative, then respond with more cooperation. Notice this is the move where it can become difficult. For those inclined to be cooperative, this is your test. You must match the competition with competition of your own. Axelrod also argues the importance of responding right away, as "if one waits to respond for un-called for defections, there is a risk of sending the wrong signal . . . [to] the other player . . . draw[ing] the conclusion that defection can pay."[9] A fast response, he says, "gives the quickest possible feedback that a defection will not pay."

3. **Forgive.** Forgiveness is a concept you don't typically associate with negotiation. But it is important. Through this process, people are going to test your limits, try to capture value from you, exert leverage over you, attempt

to deceive you, and the list could go on and on. When these things occur, it is natural to want payback. But Axelrod says if someone who has attempted to be competitive with you turns and is now willing to be cooperative, it is in your interest to forgive after responding to a provocative move.[10] This will put the negotiation on a cooperative path and lead to a better deal.

4. **Be Clear.** Finally, Axelrod says be clear.[11] Clarity around how you will manage the process leads to trust. In negotiation, I have observed that mutual trust is established when you accomplish two things. First, the other side has to know that if they are cooperative, you will also be cooperative. They have to trust that you will not take advantage of them and their cooperation. Second, the other side has to know that if they are competitive, you will also be competitive. They have to trust that they will not be able to take advantage of you and your desire to be cooperative. If you establish these two things in the course of the negotiation and make them abundantly clear for the other side, you will build the right kind of trust and incentivize the other side to be cooperative.

The key to the strategy, as Axelrod concludes, is that if "the participants know they will be dealing with each other again and again . . . [then] any attempt to exploit the [negotiation] situation will simply not pay."[12] Once this is realized, Axelrod says, "it becomes the thing to do." "If you expect others to reciprocate your defections as well as your cooperations, you will be wise to avoid starting any trouble," he wrote.[13]

Sophisticated negotiators are aware of the many strategic choices available to them. Our choices are driven by who we are negotiating with and the nature of the game we are play-ing. As you will see in the next chapter, they are also driven by what we are strategically trying to accomplish in the negotiation. Your next great negotiation outcome will be the result of your great choices in managing the process. Make them carefully.

How to Incentivize Cooperation	
Two Things the Other Side Must Believe About You	
Belief 1 If they are cooperative, you will be cooperative.	**Belief 2** If they are competitive, you will be competitive.

Build Your Framework—How to Manage Yourself in Negotiation

- Know that in every negotiation you have choices on how to approach it.
- Choose your approach by balancing the importance of the issue with the importance of the relationship.
- Avoid exploitation by using Axelrod's Four Steps to manage uncertainty.

Think It Through

- What is a competitive move you have seen recently in a negotiation? How did you respond?
- What is a cooperative move you have seen recently in a negotiation? How did you respond?

For more negotiation tools and content,
please visit negotiationmadesimple.com.

Part II
Ambitious Competition

CHAPTER FOUR

THE CHARACTERISTICS OF COMPETITIVE NEGOTIATION

If you want to change the world, don't back down from
the sharks.

—ADMIRAL WILLIAM H. McRAVEN[1]

What is competitive negotiation all about? It's a strategy used
around the world to transact business and serves as the basis
for market-driven economies. For example, fair market value
is commonly defined as "what a willing buyer will pay a willing seller." This is often determined using competitive negotiation. It's dramatic. Television shows and movies are based on
it. We see competitive negotiations covered in the news from
contract negotiations involving professional athletes to major
company acquisitions to new laws passed by a legislative body.
It's consequential. This process can influence important life
moments, such as the purchase of your first house, the sale of
your business, or securing a raise at work. The outcomes produced by competitive negotiation matter. Finally, it's predictable. Once you understand the patterns of competitive
negotiation, it becomes easier to manage toward a favorable
resolution. We'll spend the bulk of this chapter learning about

the predictable characteristics of competitive negotiation, but first we must think carefully about when to be competitive.

WHEN TO USE COMPETITIVE NEGOTIATION

Competitive negotiation is how people capture value in the world. It answers the question "Who gets how much?" This is the process used to get the things you want in life. A number of years ago, I delivered a negotiation training for the leadership team of a large engineering firm. At the end of the training, I noticed a group of engineers gather around a table in the room. They quickly engaged in a very serious and focused discussion. I had no idea what they were discussing, but it seemed important.

A few weeks later I learned about that conversation around the table at the conclusion of the training. The CEO of the engineering firm called me to give me some feedback on the training. He explained how the lessons learned about competitive negotiation encouraged one of his project teams to be more ambitious in bidding on a particular project involving the development of a stormwater management plan for a major city. They had planned on asking for 33 percent of the project, but through the course of training developed the courage to ask for more. Instead of asking for 33 percent of the project, the firm boldly asked for 50 percent of the project. Lo and behold, the firm was awarded 50 percent of the project, resulting in an additional $14 million in revenue.

This $14 million in revenue was a game changer for this engineering firm. I am sure everyone's bonus checks were a little larger that year. But even more valuable than the $14 million is the lesson learned from this experience. Here these engineers learned how to use competitive negotiation to capture more value for the firm. In this deal, they did it by simply asking for more. But the opportunity to capture more value on deals will present itself again and again, making this lesson a game changer going forward. Competitive negotiation is an incredible tool for getting more for your product or service, capturing more value in a deal, and making sure you leave nothing on the table.

It is also an important strategy to use when dealing with people who are difficult to get along with or hypercompetitive. One of the most iconic commencement speeches of the twenty-first century was delivered by retired Navy Admiral William H. McRaven at the University of Texas at Austin in 2014. The speech has generated more than fifty million views on YouTube. In the speech, Admiral McRaven offers lessons learned from Navy SEAL training as strategies for changing the world. If you need an immediate dose of inspiration, go check out the speech on YouTube.

He describes a moment in SEAL training when the candidates are flown out to San Clemente Island for a series of long swims in waters that are a breeding ground for great white sharks. Before the formidable night swim, the instructors brief the candidates on all the species of sharks that inhabit the waters but point out that, to their knowledge, no student has ever been eaten by a shark. Nevertheless, the instructors teach the candidates that if a shark begins to circle their position, they should stand their ground and not act afraid. Further, if a shark attacks, the candidates are taught to punch the shark in the snout with all their strength.

This same approach is true in life. Competitive negotiation is a tool for dealing with sharks in the business world and in life. I don't want you to get eaten alive; I want you to counter the shark's aggression with a strategic response that will make it difficult for the shark to exploit you or extract too much value in a deal. Competitive negotiation is the punch in the snout or the strategy for dealing with the sharks in your life and work.

WHY YOU NEED TO KNOW HOW TO COMPETE (EVEN IF YOU DON'T LIKE IT)

Some people are offended by the win-lose paradigm of competitive negotiation. They see striving toward mutual gain through a win-win approach as a more wholesome process that serves humankind in a better way. I recall a conversation with colleagues at a faculty dinner a few years ago. My two colleagues asked what I had covered in class that day, and I told them we studied competitive negotiation. They then asked if I thought it was productive to teach such an approach. They objected to competition philosophically and argued that it could lead to injustice and was a process too dependent on the power held by the parties. I acknowledged their points but countered with a question: What if you were appointed by a court as a guardian ad litem for a child? You got to know the child and took your responsibility for this child's well-being very seriously. As part of your duties, you monitored the child's living situation and discovered the child was the victim of abuse. The abusing parent did not want to give up custody of the child and was ready to fight in court to preserve parental rights. What would you do? Would you be cooperative with the parent, or would you fight like hell to get the child into a safer environment? In response to this situation, most people will acknowledge that justice often comes through competition, and there are moments that require a competitive approach to negotiation.

Whether you like the idea of competitive negotiation and use it regularly or prefer a more collaborative approach, the fact is that you will find yourself in competitive negotiations throughout your professional and personal life. Knowing that, let's get you ready to win!

BUYING A CAR

Buying a car is one of the most classic examples of competitive negotiation. And like most competitive negotiations, the process follows a predictable pattern. Before we go on, it's important to note that my example below covers car buying in more normal times. With a shortage of computer chips resulting from the COVID-19 pandemic and the global supply chain problems, dealers are struggling to acquire inventory and are marking up prices on vehicles. Instead of negotiating how much below the sticker price you will pay, negotiations these days determine how much above sticker price you will pay. I believe, in time, as inventory returns to normal levels, car-buying negotiations will return to their same predictable pattern. Let's examine the traditional process and see what we can learn from it.

It's a Saturday morning: You're ready to go look for a new car. You get in your old car, and when you pull into the dealership, you realize the customer parking is right in front of the showroom. As you get out of your car, you get the sense people are watching you. Well, they are! The process has already started. They usually wait for you to meander out onto the lot and settle in on a particular model, and that's when they approach you.

Let's assume it's a male salesman in this case. He comes out to meet you, and he's the friendliest person you've ever met.

He's asking all kinds of questions about your life, what you do for a living, where you work, about your family, what part of town you're from, and what kind of mileage you drive in a year. He wants you to believe he's just an interested new acquaintance, but he's not. He's sizing you up. He's already thinking about the negotiation he hopes is in the near future.

He tells you all about the car and lets you go for a test drive for ten to fifteen minutes. When you come back, he tells you to go ahead and park that new car in customer parking. And if it happens just as they hope, you'll be able to park that new car right next to your old car. They've orchestrated a moment: a way for you to compare your old life in the old car to your potential new life in the new car.

If you're interested in buying at that point, they bring you into the showroom to "talk numbers." They might try to get you to sign a bill of sale immediately, promising a "no haggle" experience (translation: no negotiation, just buy the car at their price). But if you want a better deal, you'll object to this.

The starting point of the negotiation is usually the MSRP (manufacturer's suggested retail price). As the consumer, the most important word to you in this phrase is "suggested." That's not the price of the car; it's a suggestion. Here is where the predictability becomes most rote. Say the MSRP is $40,000. You offer instead to buy it for 20 percent off that price: $32,000. The stage is set for negotiating who gets how much of the $8,000 gap that exists between their opening offer and your opening offer.

The process for closing this gap is called "the dance." The salesman is going to take off, saying he will try to work a deal. And this is where the process grows frustrating. You are left waiting in the showroom as he supposedly is talking to his manager, trying to get you a great deal on the car. But you see him chatting with another colleague in the next room or grabbing a cup of coffee. When he finally comes back to see you, he'll launch into a long explanation. Bottom line: they won't sell it for 20 percent off, but he can get you $2,000 off the MSRP.

It's a move in the right direction. But you counter with a concession of your own and raise your offer: $34,000. To this, the salesman will leave again, make you wait, and come back again, conceding another $1,000, offering it for $37,000.

Honestly, if you're lucky it will go at this pace. Often, the back-and-forth is in smaller increments: $500 or $1,000. But no matter the increments, the dance is the same. Everyone knows where the pattern is headed. It's predictable because no one wants to make a larger move than the other side.

MSRP	YOUR OFFER
$40,000	$32,000
$38,000	$34,000
$37,000	$35,000
$36,500	$35,500
$36,250	$35,750
	$36,000 Sales Price

As you get down to the end, you get frustrated and it's tempting to walk away. The process has likely taken all day. You're tired of doing math in your head. You're left arguing over a few hundred dollars to get the deal you want.

But if you're able to stay levelheaded, you will leave that night with a new car that you purchased for about $36,000.

Many people have experienced this traditional car-buying experience in the past, and they don't really like it. For this reason, many car dealers have come up with an alternative: the "no haggle price." Their solution is simply this: pay our price for the new car, and we won't make you go through the painful process of a negotiation for a deal. Everyone wins, right! But do they? Many times in negotiation, you will pay for the time you save. That might be true in the new haggle-free car-buying experience as well.

The traditional car-buying experience is a prime example of competitive negotiation. The reason it tends to be competitive is because, in the moment, you and the dealer care about the issue (the price of the car) more than the relationship. Winning the price negotiation is more important than setting the stage for a long-term friendship with the salesman. As a result, you will push for a better deal, even if it takes time and creates frustration.

The lesson to learn from the car-buying experience is that it is predictable. The best negotiators know how to use the predictability of this process to generate a favorable or fair outcome. Let me explain the predictable elements of competitive negotiation so you too can set up this process to end in your favor every time.

THE COMPETITIVE APPROACH: A PREDICTABLE PATH

Some people have the impression that a competitive approach requires lots of complicated moves or highly combative behavior designed to intimidate the other side. But fortunately, this approach is fairly straightforward and doesn't require you to bully anyone. The patterns are predictable. In just a few key moves, you can use their predictability to your own advantage.

What makes competitive negotiation predictable? There are eight characteristics:

1. **This process assumes a fixed pie.** In the example of the car, there was an $8,000 price difference between the MSRP and the original consumer offer. Once the parameters are set, you are negotiating a relatively fixed pie: $8,000.

2. **This process tends to be a zero-sum exchange.** In competitive negotiation, whatever one side gains, the other loses. In the case of the car, money is what's being negotiated. One dollar for the dealership is one dollar less in the pocket of the buyer, and vice versa.

3. **The parties are going to bargain from positions.** A position is a perspective on how the issue should be resolved. In the car-buying experience, the issue is the price of the car. The dealer's position is the MSRP, and your position is a discounted price that better meets your budget. When positions between the parties are the same, there is no need to negotiate. The deal is done. When there is a gap created by the positions, each party will have to make concessions to come to an agreement.

4. **There will be a series of concessions.** Without conceding on an original position, there will typically not be any deal. For this approach to work, each party has to be willing to do the dance and make concessions to close the gap.

5. **Each move gets smaller but takes longer to achieve.** At first, the salesperson might offer thousands of dollars in a discount, but at the end of the night you might be haggling over a few hundred dollars or something as simple as the floor mats.

6. **Negotiations gravitate toward the midpoint of the first two reasonable offers.** Even though there's a lot of back-and-forth, the outcome is usually fairly predictable: the midpoint between the first two reasonable offers. The most important word here is "reasonable." Imagine if you went into the car dealership and said, "I'll simply trade my old car worth $10,000 for your new car with an MSRP of $40,000." Your offer of a $10,000 old car for a $40,000 new car isn't reasonable, which means you can't expect to buy the car for $25,000. If you go in asking for a 20 percent discount off the MSRP, that level of discount will likely not work, but landing a 10 percent discount is more likely achievable.

7. **You can't short-circuit the dance.** The problem is that many people don't have the patience for this process. This is where the salesperson or other negotiating party will get the upper hand. When a person tries to make a quick deal, the other can use that to their advantage. If you propose at the start of the day that you skip the back-and-forth and just sign at $36,000 immediately, the salesperson will treat that as your new starting position. The fixed pie is now $4,000, and you will end up paying much closer to the MSRP than you wanted to. *Or as my late colleague Bryan Johnston liked to say, the right answer at the wrong time is the wrong answer.* As tempting as it is to try to skip this process, you just can't.

8. **Tensions increase as the process progresses.** The atmosphere will get tense. The communication may evolve from friendly and affable to contentious and testy. It will be tempting to walk away. The key is to keep your

cool, continue working the process, and you will get to the end.

HOW TO USE THE PREDICTABILITY OF COMPETITIVE NEGOTIATION TO YOUR ADVANTAGE

Predictability is what gives us an opportunity to achieve a favorable outcome and keeps us from making a very costly mistake. By understanding the predictability of competitive negotiation, you have the opportunity to manage it very well and to use this process to create great outcomes for yourself or the people you're negotiating for.

But this approach is not just about staying in it until the end (although that is a big part of it). It is about using the predictability in a disciplined way to make strategic decisions to drive a great deal. Below are four practical questions that will help you utilize the predictability of competitive negotiation.

1. How will you set up the process to close a gap in your favor? If you are responding to an opening offer, what is the gap you will create with your opening offer? If you are putting the first number on the table, what is the gap you anticipate will be created once the other side counters?

2. Is the midpoint of the anticipated gap a good place for you to do a deal?

3. As you are making concessions, does each concession hold the midpoint established by the first two reasonable offers? You may try to move the midpoint in your direction with a smaller concession, but at no point do

you want to move it in the other side's direction with a larger move.

4. How will you manage the tone and communication of the negotiation knowing competitive negotiation tends to create tension between the parties?

These four questions will create a system for managing every competitive negotiation. They will keep you from making mistakes and reveal opportunities to capture more value in a deal. The key to getting this system working for you is the opening offer. It is the most important move in all of competitive negotiation. We'll explore how to master it in the next chapter.

Build Your Framework—How to Win a Competitive Negotiation

- Understand and use the predictability of competitive negotiation.
- Be ambitious.
- Carefully craft your opening offer. It's your most important move.
- Be sure to get something you value in exchange for everything you give to the other side.
- Know that tension between you and the other side will likely emerge.
- Keep in mind the person who cares the least about the deal always has the most power.

Think It Through

- What is difficult for you about competitive negotiation? How will you manage it?
- What is easy for you about competitive negotiation? How will you use your abilities to drive a great deal?

For more negotiation tools and content,
please visit negotiationmadesimple.com.

CHAPTER FIVE

MASTER YOUR MOST IMPORTANT MOVE

You get in life what you have the courage to ask for.

—NANCY SOLOMON[1]

A number of years ago, the vice president of sales for a technology company wanted to equip his sales team with better negotiation skills, with the aim of generating more revenue for the company. He invited me to deliver a negotiation training for his sales professionals. In preparation for the training, the vice president described a common challenge many sales leaders experience with their sales teams: pressure to hit their numbers. They needed deals! To get those deals closed, the sales professionals would offer deep discounts. In doing so, they would give away the company's profit margin and make it difficult to achieve its growth expectations. Moreover, he was rightly concerned that the discounts were devaluing the product in the market and creating an expectation from customers that the quoted price was not really the price. I was tasked with helping these sales professionals think more strategically about how to get the deals without giving up all the profit.

During the training, I had the sales professionals complete a simulation demonstrating the impact of the opening offer on negotiation outcomes. This led to a conversation about their opening offers in sales negotiations. I encouraged them to think about their opening offers more strategically and consider how they could be more ambitious with their opening moves.

The sales professionals acknowledged my premise that more ambitious opening offers would produce better results, but they described a negotiation environment that would not allow them to be more ambitious. They told me how, because their market was saturated with competition, they had to seek business through a request-for-proposal process. Candidly, they admitted that their product had aged a bit and was close to being surpassed by competitors' solutions.

After a half hour of robust discussion, the vice president grew frustrated with his sales team's excuses and walked to the front of the room. He took over the class and outlined a pilot project to be commenced immediately. He instructed every member of his sales team to add 10 percent to the price quoted in the proposal. The idea was not welcome. Many voiced their opinion that such a move would significantly decrease the number of deals won and hurt the company's market share. One member of the sales team disgustedly challenged the vice president by asking, "What is the basis for the 10 percent increase?" The vice president answered assertively, "Our desire for profit!"

The pilot project was a no-risk, all-reward proposition for the sales professionals. If it crashed and burned, they had the vice president to blame for the stupid idea. If it worked, they would benefit financially through higher commissions on the more profitable deals. Despite the skepticism, the sales team fell in line and committed to asking for 10 percent more in their opening offer.

Four months later, I returned to teach an advanced course to the same group of sales professionals, and I asked the vice president about the results of the pilot project. I wanted to know how well things had worked so I could be prepared for the "I told you so" from the group. The vice president wouldn't tell me the results in advance but stated he would report the results to the entire group at the beginning of our advanced course. Here was the moment of truth. Would my premise be supported by their experience or shown to be ineffective? I was a bit nervous.

The vice president started the day of training by announcing the results of the pilot project. The sales team delivered a 3 percent increase in profitability for the company that quarter and saw no decrease in the volume of sales. It was a win for the sales team and the affirmation of a proven maxim in negotiation: people are rewarded for their ambition.

The growth the sales team produced that quarter was not the result of a refined marketing plan, an updated product, or a change in the market. Rather, profits grew by 3 percent that quarter because of how the sales team strategically handled the opening offer in their negotiations. The influence of the opening offer is real and deserves a further exploration into how we use the opening offer to set up favorable negotiation outcomes.

Let's first explore how to make your first move.

HOW TO SET THE STAGE: THE CRITICAL FIRST MOVE

The opening offer is your most important move in a competitive negotiation. Your first step to maximizing this moment is to recognize it is not a moment to be missed or passed over. The entire negotiation will proceed based on how you set up the process with your opening offer. Accordingly, this moment requires a carefully constructed strategy that sets the process up to end in your favor.

Six blunders with the opening offer and how to avoid them

In my practice, I regularly observe six costly blunders around the opening offer, including:

1. not dropping the anchor
2. putting comfort over strategy
3. using a "let's see what happens" approach
4. putting up a reasonable offer in response to an insulting offer
5. misunderstanding the purpose of the opening offer
6. starting off too aggressively

Blunder 1: Not Dropping the Anchor

Not dropping the anchor is a one-time opportunity in negotiation you do not want to miss. Anchoring is a psychological process wherein people tend to gravitate toward an initial piece of information with their goals, decisions, and expectations. It's human nature that the first proposal or piece of information you receive can become an anchor from which all other ideas are judged. Anchoring has influenced countless decisions you have made in your personal and professional life, and you probably didn't even know it.

One common example of anchoring is the prices in grocery stores and restaurants. In one famous example, Serendipity3 restaurant in New York—which has a history of marketing elaborate and very expensive versions of our favorite menu items—announced that they would be offering a $69 hot dog on their menu. According to the restaurant, the hot dog is grilled in white truffle oil, topped with duck foie gras, caramelized Vidalia onions, and black truffle Dijon mustard, and is served in a homemade pretzel bun topped with truffle butter.[2] The hot dog even made the Guinness Book of World Records for the world's most expensive hot dog.[3]

Want to order one? Most of you probably think that paying $69 for a hot dog is pretty crazy. If you do decide to splurge for one, you'll be ordering a very expensive example of an anchor. The restaurant didn't really create a $69 hot dog to try and create a popular menu item. Rather, they did so to sell more of their other menu items. Consider the $69 hot dog is likely the first thing you knew about the menu items at the restaurant. Having that as an anchor, the lesser priced (though still expensive) $17.95 cheeseburgers they sell seem like a bargain.[4] In fact, sales of the cheeseburger skyrocketed after the $69 hot dog was introduced.[5]

Anchoring can also significantly affect business decisions and negotiations. In one example, a firm searching for new office space in San Francisco set up negotiations with the building owner of the preferred space they had identified.[6] When the negotiations began, the building owner offered terms that were less than ideal—rental prices that were at the higher end of the market, a ten-year term, and annual rent increases based on inflation, among others. The negotiators for the firm responded with a relatively modest counter-proposal asking for a modest reduction in the proposed rent and a few other minor modifications to the initially proposed lease, which was quickly accepted.

Why did the negotiators ultimately go for a not-so-great lease? They were hindered by the anchor of the expensive first offer presented by the building owners. As business school professors Hammond, Keeney, and Raiffa concluded of this example in *Harvard Business Review*, "The consultants could have been much more aggressive and creative in their counter-proposal. . . . [But they] had fallen into the anchoring trap, and as a result, they ended up paying a lot more for the space than they had to."[7]

In negotiation, the first idea or proposal someone puts on the table can become the anchor simply because it is the first idea discussed. Your counterparts with differing ideas will respond based on that anchor. It happens at such a subconscious level many negotiators are not aware of psychological influence at play.

So how do we overcome anchor bias? Sourcing expert Ruzana Glaeser, writing in *Forbes*, argues that "knowledge is the best antidote to anchoring."[8] Being aware of the existence of the bias, doing good research and preparation, and mentally acknowledging and rejecting the anchor are three tips she suggests to get around the anchor.[9] And if you are caught in a discussion where the anchor has been dropped, she suggests pausing the discussion to buy time to do your own research so you can understand the true value of what is being negotiated.[10]

Another way to deal with anchors is to drop an anchor yourself. If the other side leads with an ambitious anchor, you will have to provide a counter anchor to drive the deal toward a solution that is fair and reasonable. The key is to understand the role of the anchor in the opening move and be ready to put the concept of anchoring to work for you!

Blunder 2: Putting Comfort over Strategy

A common theme that you'll read in most books and articles about negotiation centers on one of the biggest opening-offer dilemmas—who should make the first move. Making the first move is a proven way to get an advantage in a negotiation right out of the gate, but it is common for some to shy away from going first simply because they feel uncomfortable in doing so. Researchers from Duke University, the University of Michigan, and the University of Houston conducted a study to test this theory in an experiment involving graduate students making hypothetical deals with one another.[11] When asked about their emotional state during the negotiations, "[T]he negotiators who made the first offer felt more anxiety than those who did not—and, as a result, were less satisfied with their outcomes."[12] But despite their discomfort, the researchers found that "those who made the first offers did better in economic terms than those who did not."[13]

So how do you overcome this anxiety and center yourself to be comfortable making first offers, especially when it is financially advantageous to you? The researchers suggest that "some negotiators may find it helpful to role-play making the first offer and repeat this behavior in a safe simulation setting until they feel comfortable enacting it in a real-world situation."[14] I recommend talking with a trusted colleague or a wise friend about your opening offer strategy plan so they can either steer you in a different direction or give you the courage to ambitiously pursue your deal starting with the first move. The affirmation of another will often be all you need to overcome the anxiety of making an ambitious opening offer. As negotiation expert Carol Frohlinger says, "Don't bargain yourself down before you get to the table."[15]

Blunder 3: Using a "Let's See What Happens" Approach

People take a "let's see what happens" approach with their opening offers and do not commit to an opening offer strategy. As a result, they end up being influenced by the other side's opening offer. As a young lawyer, I was assigned a slip-and-fall case. Upon receiving the file, I investigated by interviewing all the relevant parties. My client was an insurance company that provided coverage for this claim. I called the claims professional at the insurance company to let her know I had concluded my investigation and it was my opinion that liability did exist and the case should be settled.

I asked her if I could commence early-settlement negotiations with plaintiff's counsel. She said no because the file was not yet complete. I then asked what information the file needed for it to be considered complete. She indicated that I needed to get a demand from the plaintiff's counsel to complete the file. Frustrated by this process, I decided to conduct a mini experiment to see what the impact of the demand from plaintiff's counsel would be. I asked her to give me her opinion as to the settlement value of this claim. She stated that based on everything she reviewed and her experience with similar claims, this claim was worth around $35,000. I penciled that number on the top of the file folder.

As instructed, I called the plaintiff's counsel and requested a demand package. He was more than happy to oblige. When the demand package arrived a week or so later, it contained a demand of $300,000. I submitted the information to the company and waited to hear back. About ten days later, the claims

professional called me to tell me that I was authorized to commence early-settlement negotiations. To my surprise, she indicated I had $75,000 of authority to settle the case. I carefully
asked how the authority rose to $75,000 on a case she thought
was worth $35,000. She stated that based on the plaintiff's
counsel demand, the claims committee believed it would take
more than $35,000 to settle the case.

This little experiment reinforced the power of the opening
offer. The authority given was over twice what the claims professional believed to be the value of the claim. The piece of
information that influenced the claims committee to increase
the amount of authority was the plaintiff's opening offer. If
this were a boxing match and I was judging the fight, I would
say plaintiff's counsel won round one of this fight.

Blunder 4: Putting Up a Reasonable Offer in Response to an Insulting Offer

I was recently engaged to provide some counsel for the buyer
in a business-acquisition negotiation. The company looking
to be acquired put forth an asking price of $8 million, which
was substantially higher than any objective valuation of the
business. The buyer completed due diligence and determined
the business was worth around $5 million. Acting on the val-
uation, the buyer offered $5 million to acquire the company.
The buyer believed this offer was reasonable and supported by
the valuation of the business. In response, the company low-
ered its price to $7 million and put forth its own valuation
generated by one of its consultants. Now the buyer was stuck!
They were prepared to offer up to $5.5 million for the com-
pany, which they determined would be a slight overpayment
but a good deal in the long term. Anything more than $5.5
million would be an overpayment.

Do you see the problem? The buyer is hoping to get $2.5 million in concessions with only $500,000. That'll be tough. The problem was created when the buyer responded to an insulting opening offer ($8 million) with a reasonable opening offer ($5 million). If the buyer wanted to purchase the company for $5.5 million, it should have responded to the $8 million offer with a more aggressive offer of $3 million to $4 million—creating a midpoint at around $5.5 million rather than $6.5 million established by its more reasonable offer. That one wrong move may cost the buyer hundreds of thousands of dollars in acquiring this company, or it may mean the deal does not happen at all. As you will recall from chapter 4, the right answer at the wrong time is the wrong answer.

Blunder 5: Misunderstanding the Purpose of the Opening Offer

So many people believe your opening position functions as a first attempt to reach a deal. But in competitive negotiation, it actually serves other strategic functions. The opening position has five roles:

1. **It starts the dance.** Trying to shortcut the dance doesn't work. Giving an opening offer will get you started on the necessary process.
2. **It drops the anchor.** As we've discussed, it sets the parameters of the fixed pie, creating a pull toward a better median outcome for you.
3. **It manages the expectations of the other side.** From the outset, they know what kind of deal you're looking to make.
4. **It gives you a chance to get a great deal.** We never get what we don't ask for. By starting with an ambitious

opening position, you create a possibility for the other side to concede early and for you to obtain even more than you originally hoped.

5. **It puts you in the driver's seat.** The opening position gives you control over the outcome of the situation.

Blunder 6: Starting Off Too Aggressively

While most of the conversation around opening offer mistakes involves being too generous, one can also be too aggressive. If you are negotiating with a disciplined negotiator, this may result in the other party walking away from the negotiation or abandoning the pursuit of the deal altogether.

Just because the other side doesn't like your opening offer, that doesn't mean it is too aggressive. Competitive negotiators who are skilled in responding to an opening offer will act offended by the number in an effort to get you to put more money on the table in your next move. The real test is whether the other side responds at all. If they walk after your opening move, it may be too aggressive. If they provide a counteroffer, you are now in the game.

The downside of starting off too aggressively is it may incite competition. An aggressive opening offer may cause someone who is ready to be reasonable to become much more competitive as a means of protecting themselves or as an emotional response to your move. When people are threatened, they often get aggressive or angry. An aggressive opening offer can be counterproductive to achieving the best outcome in the negotiation.

The latest research suggests that while an aggressive opening offer may try to show your competitor just how tough you are, it could actually backfire if you try to drive too hard a bargain. Researchers from the University of Technology,

Sydney, conducted an experiment in which a group of players exchanged offers for a share of $10, simulating a typical negotiating process.[16] They found that success depended not only on the opening offer but also on the dynamic that developed during the bargaining process following the opening offer. An aggressive opening offer was often met with a negative, and even spiteful, counteroffer.

It really is all about threading the needle to get the best final outcome. As the researchers suggest, "[T]o strike a good bargain, your opening offer needs to be not too hard, or you risk a spiteful counteroffer, but not too soft either, or you might be taken for a ride." Let's explore a simple approach for constructing highly effective opening offers.

NAIL THE OPENING OFFER BY ANSWERING THREE STRATEGIC QUESTIONS

As you prepare for the most important move in the entire process, ask yourself three questions.

1. **Who is going to make the first offer?** There are only two options here: you make the first offer or the other side does. What you're weighing here is the value of information versus influence. When you let the other person make the first move, you get *information* on where they stand and what they're hoping to get. But by making the first offer yourself, you have more influence over the result. My advice is to capture as much influence as possible by stating your position first.

2. **Where are you going to start?** You can either take an extreme position or a reasonable one. An extreme position gives you the flexibility to concede and manages the

expectations of the other side. They will have to adjust their expectation of the result. A reasonable opening may be the right option in a case when you don't have a lot of time to go back and forth. If making a reasonable offer, provide as much information as possible about why the offer is reasonable.

3. **How are you going to make the opening offer?** You can be firm on your opening stance or soft about it. A soft offer pairs well with an extreme one. If you are too firm on an extreme price, people will despair and walk away. If your opening price is reasonable, then you'll have to be firm about it if you're going to walk away with a fair deal.

RESPONDING TO AN OPENING OFFER

Responding to an opening offer is a critically important moment in the negotiation process that doesn't get much attention. The other side will make decisions on their next move based on your reaction to their opening offer. On the next page is a table that outlines strategic responses to an opening offer from the other side:

OTHER SIDE'S OPENING OFFER	YOUR PREFERRED RESPONSES
AGREEMENT ZONE	• Make good progress. • Look to capture more value. • Strike the deal.
CREDIBLE ZONE	• Manage expectations with your behavior, communication, and counteroffer. • Communicate concessions that will need to be made to get a deal. • Counter with an offer in your credible zone.
INSULT ZONE	• Must communicate in your style that you are insulted. • Consider what message you want to send with your opening number. • Do not put a reasonable offer on the table in response to an insulting offer.

DON'T GET PLAYED WITH THE OPENING OFFER

Let me close with a story about an experience my friend had with his fifteen-year-old daughter, Courtney, as she planned for prom. She was only a sophomore in high school at that point, but she was popular, and her parents weren't surprised that she was asked to the senior prom. But they were also concerned about her curfew, and they wanted to set a good precedent for future years. They knew a negotiation was coming up. They sat down together before meeting with Courtney and agreed that while her curfew was normally 11:00 p.m., they'd let her stay out until midnight.

But when Courtney came to them with her request, they were taken completely by surprise. Courtney made the first move. She told them all about the agenda for the night: At 4:00 p.m., they would gather for hair, makeup, and photos, then go to dinner and on to the dance. She told them the dance ends at 11:00 p.m. and that the plan was to go to one friend's house for a campfire, then another friend's house for movies, then to drive to the beach to watch the sunrise. The whole event would end with a trip to the Original Pancake House for waffles. She told them she'd be home by 9:00 a.m. My friend and his wife were stunned. His wife, in a fury, made a firm counteroffer, saying, "I want to be crystal clear. There is no way you're staying out past 2:00 a.m." The wife stormed out, and then Courtney did, too, yelling and screaming about how her parents were just mean and how unfair it was that her friends got to stay out and have fun and she had to come home.

My friend took a minute to process what had just occurred in his kitchen. He was a sophisticated negotiator, having served as a state legislator and the president of two universities. He spent the next several hours restoring peace between his wife and daughter. And then, a few days later, he learned that he and his wife had been played. He overheard a conversation between Courtney and her friend on the phone. Courtney was ecstatic and amazed that she was given permission to stay out until 2:00 a.m. She exclaimed, "I can't believe it worked! I can't believe I got 2:00 a.m." In that moment, my friend chuckled as he realized his fifteen-year-old daughter had just out-negotiated him through her strategic use of the opening offer.

The most important move in competitive negotiation is your first move. If you don't do it right, it will cost you. If you do it right, you can achieve more than you every thought possible. Just ask Courtney!

Build Your Framework—How to Nail the Opening Offer

- Determine where you want to end the negotiation.
- Develop an opening offer that will launch the process and give you the best chance of ending the negotiation at your preferred outcome.
- Know the purpose of the opening offer is not to get a deal in that moment but to set expectations.
- Practice your delivery. Be sure if it is extreme, it is soft. If it is reasonable, it must be firm.

Think It Through

- What circumstance have you bargained yourself down before ever making the opening offer? What was the result? What would you do differently with your new knowledge and skill?
- What are creative ways you can manage your fear of the other side walking away if your opening offer is too aggressive?

For more negotiation tools and content, please visit negotiationmadesimple.com.

CHAPTER SIX

CONCEDE WITH PURPOSE

We must be courageous but also reasonable.

—LECH WALESA[1]

One of my mentors, Peter, tells a story about buying a suite of furniture for his master bedroom. He and his wife, Vicki, were about to celebrate their thirtieth wedding anniversary. Peter asked Vicki what she wanted to do to celebrate this marriage milestone. To Peter's surprise, Vicki exclaimed that she wanted brand-new, top-of-the-line bedroom furniture for their master bedroom. She pointed out that during their entire marriage, they had never slept on a bed they had purchased new for themselves.

Peter and Vicki headed down to a high-end furniture store to look for bedroom furniture. They found a bedroom suite they loved and then began discussing price with the sales associate. Once everything was added up, the grand total for the bedroom furniture came to just more than $12,000. Peter, a mediator and expert in negotiation, began to go to work. He asked the sales associate if that was the best price and let him know he would need a deal to pull the trigger on the purchase.

The sales associate said, "Sir, we don't negotiate. I have no authority to offer any discounts on this furniture." Peter picked up on the authority reference and asked to speak to the manager. The manager sat down with Peter and explained how the company does not negotiate but competitively prices its furniture. He showed them an invoice of a purchase for more than $90,000 of furniture and pointed out that there was no discount given on a purchase of that size, not even a throw pillow. Now frustrated, Peter and Vicki left the store that day feeling wholly unsatisfied about having to pay full retail price for the furniture.

For the next several days, Peter and Vicki visited other furniture stores but didn't find anything they liked. Peter then got the idea to call other stores that carried the same furniture. He found other stores with that furniture but could not get a better price. As Peter says, "I could not beat the system." The retail pricing was locked in no matter which store he used to purchase the furniture.

Despite not being able to get a deal, Peter and Vicki decided to splurge and purchase the furniture. They went back to the original store and the original sales associate. They processed the transaction for a little more than $12,000 and right before the end of the paperwork, the sales associate paused. He reached over and pulled what looked like a marker from his desk. He asked them if there was any chance the furniture might get scratched in their home. They said, "Yes, of course." He then described the marker as the exact color of the finish of the new furniture. If it got scratched, all they had to do was touch it up with this marker, and they would never see it. Peter said, "We'll take it," thinking he was finally going to get something out of the deal. The sales associate said, "Great. The cost is $14.99. I'll add it to the deal."

Peter was flabbergasted. He spent more than $12,000, and the furniture store wouldn't throw a $15 marker into the deal. They finished the transaction and left the store. As they sat in their car in the parking lot, Peter asked Vicki how she felt. She mentioned how she loved the furniture but felt like they got ripped off. Peter knew he had to do something. He wanted his bedroom to be a happy place and did not want to revisit negative feelings about the furniture every time he or Vicki entered the room. Therefore, Peter proposed that they consider this a no-expense-spared gift to each other. For once, they spent what they had to spend to get exactly what they wanted. But that wasn't all. Peter and Vicki were still looking for psychological satisfaction, so they resorted to self-help. Because the store refused to make any concessions and give them any sense of a win in the deal, Peter and Vicki vowed to each other to never purchase another item from this furniture store ever again. The resentment built up through how this negotiation was handled didn't cost the furniture store this deal, but it cost the furniture store any future business. As you will recall from earlier in the book, one of the skills of great negotiators is that they know how to satisfy all the parties.

Peter's story reveals the importance of concessions in the negotiation process. Concessions play three important roles. First, the importance of how value is exchanged and the moves that are needed for the parties to reach an agreement cannot be understated. Second, they are communication devices that carry important signals to each party useful for managing expectations and determining how a deal might happen. Third, they are an important part of the psychological game that underlies the negotiation. Knowing these roles will help you develop a strategy for managing concessions so you come out the winner. But let's go further. Let's explore how we can use carefully constructed concessions to get a great deal for ourselves *and* make the other side feel good about it.

There are seven tools the best negotiators use to manage concessions:

1. Set up the process.
2. Always keep the end in mind.
3. Let the deal come to you.
4. Manage perceptions.
5. Create a *win* for the other side.
6. Say no.
7. Use linkage.

Tool 1: Set Up the Process.

The key to an outstanding concession strategy is setting it up properly. This brings us back to the opening offer. Are you convinced yet that the opening offer is the most important move in a competitive negotiation? An extreme opening offer that creates a gap with the other side will position you to make some very substantial concessions. As I will explain in just a few sections, this sets up the perceived win for the other side— even though you have set up the process to deliver a very good deal for you. If you do not leave yourself enough room to move, the other side may perceive you using a take-it-or-leave-it approach to negotiation. This approach creates a sense of losing for the party that is compelled to make that decision.

One of my clients is a US-based organization that operates globally. They invited me to train their lead negotiators on cross-cultural negotiation. During the training, it was clear that these negotiators had developed a reputation for being arrogant. They explained how people perceived them as my-way-or-the-highway negotiators. The irony was that they were going to extreme measures to ensure their deals were considered fair on the global market. In fact, the organization was hiring economists to evaluate their deals to affirm that they were fair and reasonable according to an objective, arm's-length standard.

I asked them how the desire to be perceived as tough was affecting their negotiation behavior. They referred back to the opening offer and mentioned how they always started as reasonable as possible based on the recommendation of the third-party economist. I then asked how many times the other side opened in the zone of agreement. The answer was never. I followed by asking what they did in this circumstance. They said they held firm to their number or only made very small concessions because they didn't allow themselves much room to move.

We then had a great discussion about the other side's perceptions when they laid down an offer and refused to move. I gently suggested that it was the process, not the substance, that was shaping the reputation they so despised. To change it, they had to actually start with more aggressive opening offers to leave room to make larger concessions. This would create the perception that the organization is willing to be reasonable with its partners and is making sacrifices to reach a deal.

The key to an effective concession strategy is setting it up to succeed. This is done through your opening offer.

Tool 2: Always Keep the End in Mind.

The formation of the concession strategy should be based on your target deal. It is all about how you are going to close the gap between your opening offer and your target deal or, in the worst case, your bottom line. For the process to work, two things must occur. First, your target deal must be somewhat reasonable. A process set up to deliver a deal that is unreasonably ambitious will likely fail. Second, once you have determined your target, every move should be tested against whether the deal is headed in that direction. The best point of reference is the midpoint of each round of the negotiation. If the midpoint is close to your target deal, you are probably on track. If the midpoint and your target deal are not close, it is probably time for a shift in strategy.

Tool 3: Let the Deal Come to You.

It's natural to want to get a deal done quickly. But, if you are willing to take your time and make smaller concessions, you will be in a position to capture more value. With this approach, you will be tested. You will create tension. Your process will be challenged. And, you will need intestinal fortitude to overcome some of the tactics and threats thrown at you by the other side. But if you stay disciplined, many deals will move in your direction, and you will win the day.

Tool 4: Manage Perceptions.

You may have heard the saying "Perception is reality." This is true in many negotiations. Perceptions become reality because decisions are often based on perceptions held by the parties. Let me share with you an example. It is the perception of winning and losing. People who perceive themselves as winning tend to be more conservative and want to hold on to that which they have won. People who perceive themselves as losing tend to be willing to take more risks because they feel like they have nothing more to lose.

I have observed that really sophisticated negotiators work to give the other side a perception of winning when in reality they are losing. My friend Peter Robinson calls this "good manners in negotiation." It is bad manners to celebrate the deal in the presence of the other side and make them believe they got a bad deal. Instead, you want to give them a sense that they are winning as the process progresses. The way you do this is to express reluctance and difficulty in making concessions. In other words, feign pain. Your expression may be in the time it takes for you to make your next move, it may be in the process you need to work through to make a next concession, or it may be in the way you communicate the next move. The other side must believe that each move is becoming increasingly difficult for you. If they sense your concessions are easy, savvy negotiators will become competitive and look to capture even more value.

By managing perceptions well, you can make the other side feel good about a deal that in reality is good for you! Let the other side have the perceived victory so long as you take home the actual victory.

Tool 5: Create a *Win* for the Other Side.

J. Paul Getty was a twentieth-century oil tycoon and, at one time, the richest living American. You may know him as the namesake of the spectacular art museum that sits above the 405 freeway just north of Los Angeles. He once shared a lesson from his father, who said, "You must never try to make all the money in a deal. Let the other fellow make some money too, because if you have a reputation for always making all the money, you won't have many deals."[2] This lesson is important for negotiators. It is important to remember that you want the other side to experience a win in the deal, whether it is real or perceived. You obviously do not want that win to come at your expense, but you want to help the other side find a way to win, too.

I have learned that any business arrangement that is not profitable to the other side will in the end become problematic for me. It is the deals that generate satisfaction on both sides that tend to be more durable and are likely to be repeated.

Tool 6: Say No.

Do you remember buying your first car? My wife, Melissa, and I had just finished business school and law school, respectively. We were both employed and living the DINK (Double Income, No Kids) lifestyle. She was still driving a fifteen-year-old Honda Accord with 160,000+ miles on it at the time. It was one of those models with the automatic seat belts—one of the most annoying innovations in automotive history. We both decided it was time for a new car.

Melissa already knew what she wanted. I set out to find her the perfect car at a great price. My process began with telephone calls to sales managers at dealerships across the region. I asked them if they had the car my wife wanted and what their best price was. I told them I would go to the dealership that gave me the best price over the phone. Some of the dealerships refused to give me a price over the phone, but I got three dealerships into the game. After each call, I would call the other dealerships back and tell them they were no longer the lowest price and had to lower their price to get me in the door.

It finally came down to a two-horse race. The dealership in second place said the dealership with the lowest price was setting me up. It was a bait and switch. There was no way they could sell me the car at that price without some additional fees. True to my word, I drove the old Honda down to the winning dealership. There I met an assistant sales manager. Let's call him Chuck. I told Chuck that I needed another $500 off the price of the car because the other dealership told me to be aware of the bait and switch. He denied the use of any such tactic but left to go see what he could do. To my surprise, Chuck eventually returned and told me he would throw another $500 into the deal if it meant doing the deal today.

I then let Chuck know that I wanted to trade in the old Honda and told him I needed $2,500 out of the trade-in to make the numbers work. Chuck sent it through the appraisal process and came back and said that was really too much to pay for the Honda, but he would do it if it meant doing the deal that day. We then started talking about financing. I thought that's where Chuck was going to get me. I told Chuck I was preapproved at my credit union at 4.7 percent. If he could beat it, I would finance with him. We filled out the application and Chuck came back ready to finance the car at 4.3 percent.

How would you be feeling at this point? If you are like my wife, you are feeling great. She said, "Let's do the deal and get out of here." But I wasn't ready. Something wasn't sitting right with me. The deal was too easy, which made me think I wasn't getting a very good deal. Instead of feeling great, I was nervous, but didn't have anything left to talk about. Chuck had said yes to my every request.

The only thing I knew to do was grab an accessories brochure. I asked Melissa to pick out something she wanted to go with her new car. She thought I was crazy, but she pointed to the trunk mat. I called Chuck back over and told him the car needed a trunk mat. He was surprised that that was what was holding up the deal, but I insisted. To my surprise, about ten minutes later Chuck showed up with the trunk mat under his arm. He said, "Mr. Lowry, here is your trunk mat. Do we have a deal?" Now, you will think I am crazy, but my answer was no. As you can imagine, Chuck was now growing frustrated with me.

I asked my wife to pick out something else from the accessories brochure. She quickly selected the fog lights. I informed Chuck that there was a "safety issue" with the vehicle. He was flabbergasted. He exclaimed, "It's a brand-new car. There's no safety issue." I told him my wife's eyesight wasn't great and we needed fog lights. Giving me a frustrated look, Chuck stormed off. About thirty minutes later, Chuck came back to tell me that to install the fog lights they would have to remove the front bumper of the car. He said that would be a $700 job, but that he would do it for $350. He then said, "That's it. Do you want the car or not?" At that moment, I told Chuck to forget the fog lights and write up the deal for the car.

What did I need from Chuck? It may seem counterintuitive, but I needed a no. Why? Because that's the only way I would know that I got the best deal possible. In competitive negotiation, sometimes the best way to get the other side to say yes is to say no. They need to know you have reached your bottom line and they have extracted all the value possible in the deal. Strategic negotiators carefully plan when they are going to say no and use this response as a way to get the other side to do the deal.

Tool 7: Use Linkage.

So what happens if you come to a place where no one wants to concede? What if you come to an impasse, where neither party seems willing to budge?

The secret is in the use of one two-letter word: *if*.

If: we see this word everywhere and likely don't even notice it. That's how expected it is in negotiation. For example, think about the last time you gave your email address away on a web page. Likely, you gave it to receive a "free" article, video, or sample of some kind. But it wasn't free. What the company said was: "If you give us your email address, we will give you something in return."

That's a classic example of linkage. Linkage is the act of strategically connecting various pools of value in a negotiation. Linkage is such a valuable tool because it ensures you *get* value in exchange for the value that you *give*. This can bring progress to a stalled negotiation.

For example, one CEO I worked with was trying to close the largest deal in the history of the firm. It was a marketing package for a professional sports franchise. Although eager to make the deal, the franchise wouldn't agree to the firm's price. Instead of just giving up the price for the sake of landing a big client, the CEO used that two-letter word: *if*. He came up with seven things that "if" the franchise would do them, he would make the final concession on price. These things were valuable to the firm but cost the franchise almost nothing: PR activity, endorsements, and so on. To the CEO's surprise, the franchise quickly agreed to all seven stipulations.

In this case, by linking things that were valuable to the firm but weren't very sacrificial for the franchise, with what the franchise actually wanted (a lower price), they were able to come to an agreement. The opposite can also be done: link concessions that are valuable to the other party (but not that sacrificial for you) to elements that you actually do want.

This creativity in the midst of a competitive negotiation moves you past a block.

There are of course limitations to the competitive approach—which I'll detail in the next chapter. But for any of its flaws, competitive negotiation is predictable: if you dance the dance, you can have relative certainty about where you'll end up. So when you're in a negotiation that requires competition, don't forget to use the power of your opening offer and linkage to your advantage. These might seem like small moves but are what make the biggest difference in where the negotiation lands.

A LAST WORD ON COMPETITIVE NEGOTIATION

By now, some of you reading this book might be growing anxious about managing competitive negotiations. Making an ambitious opening offer or only making a small concession is hard because it is not what the other side wants you to do. They want you to make a generous opening offer and use large concessions to get to a deal. This clearly will shift the exchange of value in their direction, making it a smooth process to a deal. The only problem is, it won't be a very good deal.

On the other hand, when you are competitive it creates tension. The other party will be frustrated and at times even angry when the deal doesn't move in their direction. They will take an extreme position themselves or push back on your moves. The conversation may grow intense, and at times it can become personal as emotions come into play.

Most of us spend our lives trying to avoid such conflict. It is true in some cases that the conflict can be so costly, it doesn't warrant a competitive approach to negotiation. You never want to win the battle but lose the war. But many people use this line of thinking as a rationale for not doing what strategically needs to be done in a competitive negotiation. As we close this section on competitive negotiation, let me give you a strategy for dealing with the discomfort you may experience. It involves substance and style (see figure 3).

Let's start with substance. This is the value being exchanged. Throughout this section, I have argued that there is value to be claimed if you are more ambitious and make slower and smaller moves throughout the concession process. This is being competitive on substance. You can also be cooperative on substance. This is where you are generous with your opening offer and willing to make larger concessions to get to a quick and easy deal.

Now let's turn to style. A competitive style is marked by hostile communication, threats, personal attacks, temper tantrums, the use of leverage, a nasty worded email, or a take-it-or-leave-it approach. All these behaviors are designed to make you crack. The hope is you will give value to avoid the tension created by the other side when you make a move they do not like.

A cooperative style is one where the communication is professional, the atmosphere is friendly and hopeful, the messages are measured and respectful, and the process stays focused on getting to an agreement. All of the personal attacks and bad behavior are left for another day.

Here's the trick! I have observed many highly effective negotiators who are competitive on the substance but cooperative in style. This is a great approach for getting a deal but also for maintaining a strong relationship. It is useful for negotiations with clients, employees, colleagues, and others with whom you need a positive, healthy relationship despite the current negotiation. What this means for you is that you don't have to be a jerk. You don't have to change anything about how you behave, communicate, or interact with others. You can be friendly, professional, and respectful. What I am suggesting is that you simply make more careful and strategic decisions in how you give away value in this process. Being competitive on substance while employing a cooperative style is a powerful combination to use when managing competitive negotiation.

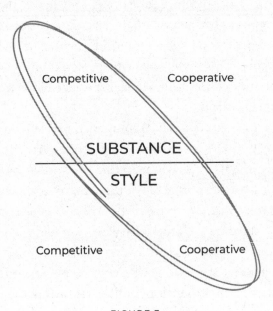

FIGURE 3

Build Your Framework—How to Manage Concessions

- View concessions as opportunities to capture value from the other side. Be sure the value you capture is worth the concession required to get it.
- Give yourself room to make concessions by using an ambitious opening offer.
- Don't be a jerk; just be disciplined in how to give value in the negotiation. You can be personable, reasonable, and tough at the same time.
- Go slow and make small moves. Some of the best deals take time to construct.
- Know there will always be pressure to give more and do more to get a deal. Counter this pressure with pressure of your own on the other side.
- Don't forget you can walk away. If the deal isn't coming together like you want it, you can always shut down the process.
- Remember, competitive negotiation usually ends at the midpoint of the first two reasonable offers.

Think It Through

- How will you handle the pressure from the other side to concede in negotiation?
- How will you deliver pressure to the other side to concede in negotiation?

For more negotiation tools and content,
please visit negotiationmadesimple.com.

Part III
Creative Cooperation

CHAPTER SEVEN

TRANSITION FROM POSITIONS

Let us move from the era of confrontation to the era
of negotiation.

—RICHARD NIXON[1]

A competitive approach is useful if we have power in the negotiation. But there are moments when we *don't* have a lot of power, and the other person has the upper hand. In these cases, we're not going to be successful by being competitive. In this case, the best approach is a creative, cooperative one.

WHEN COMPETITION FAILS YOU

Let me tell you about my very first case as a lawyer.

One of the partners came over to my desk, handed me a big file, and told me to start reading. The files told a story about a woman who had gone to the emergency room for difficulty breathing. After running tests and doing a full respiratory workup, the doctors decided she had only a cold. There was not much to do, but they kept her overnight for observation, just to be safe.

When taking her to her overnight room, the health care workers had to transfer her from the gurney to the bed: one person at her head and one at her feet. Here is where the accident happened: the woman claimed that one worker wasn't quite strong enough for the move, and in the transfer, as he lunged to get her into the bed, he lost his balance and fell on her. After the fall, she claimed to have complained immediately about pain through her back and torso.

But the medical records didn't show a record of complaints. When her physician decided to do a scan prior to discharge, it revealed two compression fractures in her back.

The partner and I asked her attorney if we could hear her story, and we arranged a visit. The woman told us her story clearly and in detail. And the attorney I was working with asked her a reasonable question: What will it take to get this resolved?

Her answer surprised me: First, she wanted to make sure things were being done safely and correctly at that hospital. She had worked as a nurse for a long time, and she knew that for a woman of her size, there should be at least three to do a transfer. Second, she wanted an apology. She called herself "old school," saying that if you hurt someone, even if you didn't mean to, you should apologize. She was frustrated that no one at the hospital even acknowledged what had happened. Last, she wanted to be able to keep returning to that hospital, as that's where her physician had privileges.

A little confused, my colleague asked the same question again, receiving the same response.

Finally, the woman's lawyer interrupted, saying they were demanding $150,000 to resolve the case.

We could immediately see that the hospital's position was not looking great: The woman's story was straightforward and credible. She would make a sympathetic witness in front of a jury. We knew that a competitive approach would likely favor the woman's initial position of $150,000—an amount her lawyer had set firmly.

Those three requests stuck with me. When the litigation manager from the hospital showed up for the mediation several months later, he asked me for the overview of what was really going on, and I gave him the woman's three requests. He took those and he ran with it. During the meeting he gave the following speech:

"Ma'am, I care about you. You haven't even sued my hospital yet, and here I am, showing up and trying to resolve this case. But I need you to understand that I can only resolve it for a reasonable amount. But if we can get to where we both can be reasonable with each other, I think we can get this done today.

"Ma'am you also need to know that when things go wrong in this hospital, it is usually me that has to deal with it. You have my word that I'm going to go back and make sure we're doing the right things as they relate to bed transfers.

"Here's another thing I want you to know: I'm deeply sorry for the experience that you had at our hospital, not only for the lack of care that you received but for the fact that we didn't acknowledge what you told us. So as I make decisions today, I'm going to make my decisions based upon your story. And based upon what you say happened because I believe you.

"Ma'am, I also want you to know that we're honored to have you as one of our patients. And if you ever need medical care again, I hope you'll come back to let us care for you."

At this, the woman cried.

We settled the case later in the day for far less than the original demand.

What this story reveals is that the intangible—what is going on below the surface—matters. The intangible is very, very powerful.

What do you do when you're at a disadvantage? The solution is not to turn competitive but to take a cooperative approach that relies on a key ingredient: the interests driving both sides in the negotiation.

THE ANATOMY OF A DEAL

There are moments when we need to be competitive and claim value, but then there are moments when cooperation works even better. Cooperative negotiation aims to understand and creatively meet the needs of everybody involved. It's a process of creating value.

As demonstrated in the hospital injury case, cooperative negotiation involves intangibles that you often, but not always, find in negotiation: for the injured patient, the intangibles were a guarantee of better protocols, an apology for the incident, and a warm welcome in the future.

Let's explore this using a diagram that I call the Anatomy of a Deal:

Issue

The need for a deal begins with a problem, complex or simple, that the parties are looking to solve.

Position ⬅ Issue ➡ Position

Positions are perspectives on how the issue should be resolved. If those positions align, then the negotiation is easy. But that is rarely the case. When each party has different ideas about how the issue should be resolved—when each holds a different position—they often spend a lot of time and energy trying to convince the other side their position is correct.

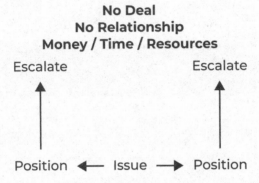

As you can see from the diagram, this leads to an escalation, potentially no deal at all, damaged relationships, and wasted time, money, and resources. It's not very effective.

But understanding the collaborative approach will help you create new value where there wasn't value before. This new tactic will transform who you are as a negotiator and exponentially increase your ability to close deals. It's three simple words: transition from positions. These are perhaps the most important words in all of negotiation!

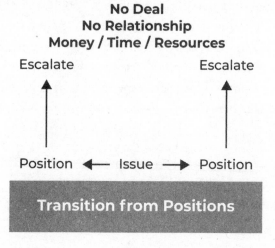

Where do you go with the conversation when you transition from positions? When you transition from issues and positions to interests you will find things like:

- egos
- fears
- motives
- values
- goals
- relationships
- circumstances

On this diagram, we call them interests: what a person is truly interested in gaining, protecting, or developing.

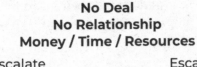

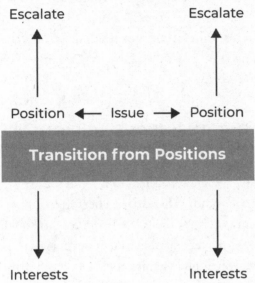

Let's explore the difference between interests and positions. Positions are concrete. You can divide them or negotiate them. They are the prize. They are specific stipulations. They are rights and privileges. They are terms of a deal. Interests are what a person truly cares about. They are intangible. They can't be measured or divided. They are often hard to identify or articulate. But these are the things that cause a person or party to take a position.

When you transition from positions, you get insight into the other party's real interests. And when you see what another person really wants, you are better able with information to orchestrate a creative solution that satisfies everyone's true desires.

This principle is not just true in negotiation: it's true in business and on an interpersonal level. What happens to companies that best understand their customers' needs and are the most creative in meeting those needs? They are highly successful industry leaders. What happens when friends or spouses actually listen to each other and act on below-the-surface interests? Relationships flourish. That's the power of transitioning from positions. Let's explore how it plays out in the business world.

HOW MOST BUSINESS DECISIONS ARE MADE

For decades, researchers have been studying why consumers stay loyal to a brand. What drives a person to do business with one company over another? What the researchers found was that about 30 percent of these business decisions were made based on reason, logic, or some form of quantitative analysis.[2] So it invites an obvious question. What were the other 70 percent of decisions based on? The answer: emotion.[3] People make decisions every day that do not make any logical sense, but it makes them feel good, so they go for it. To illustrate, as I write this, I am sitting in a slammed Starbucks in Nashville. Everyone in this coffeehouse could have found a cheaper cup of coffee this morning. It really doesn't make sense that they would pay Starbucks prices for coffee until you understand that consumer decisions are largely based on emotion, not logic or analysis. The reason this Starbucks is making a fortune this morning is because the Starbucks experience makes people feel good at the start of their day.

This research explains why transitioning from positions is so powerful in negotiation. Even in the context of commercial business transactions, people are going to make most decisions based on emotion. It's not what they *think* about the deal, it's how they *feel* about the deal. The best negotiators know the importance of embracing the emotional elements involved in negotiation and creatively responding in a way that makes people feel good about deals.

Let me take this phenomenon one step further. In my years of practice as a professional negotiator, I have learned that people are not driven by their impression of me, my position, or the product I am selling. What seems more significant to their decision-making process is how they feel about themselves when considering doing business with me. Did you catch the nuance? Notice the decision driver here is ego. They want to look good as a result of purchasing the product, acquiring the business, or signing up for the service. Therefore, my job as a negotiator is to use a process in which they can feel good about themselves when they say yes and do the deal. By an objective standard, that deal may not be a great deal, but if the other side *feels* good about themselves, it will likely get done. This is why people overpay for coffee, cars, houses, and so on.

If you are in business, this realization is an opportunity to transform how you engage your customer. How many of the slides in your presentation are about your company or your product? How many of your slides are about the potential customer and making them look good in how you will solve their problem? Transitioning from positions means engaging your customer and positioning your product or service as a way for them to look good. As my friend Don Miller says in his book *Building a StoryBrand*, it is solving both their *external* problem and their *internal* problem.[4]

In 2022, I founded a management consulting firm called Thrivence, based in Nashville, Tennessee. My colleagues have embraced the idea that while we are hired to solve business and technology problems, our success really depends on whether we make the person who hired us look good. Whether it's a CEO wanting to look good for her employees or a manager wanting to look good for his vice president, this is the internal problem of leaders we are asked to help solve every day through our solutions. I believe this is true not only for our business but for yours as well. It is the empathetic business leaders and negotiators who will set themselves apart in the twenty-first century. They will win the business, make the fortunes, and change the world.

WORKING WITH FORMIDABLE PEOPLE

Transitioning from positions is also a useful strategy for dealing with formidable people. As a negotiator, you will encounter all kinds of people, personalities, and positions. Inevitably, you will find yourself having to negotiate around a problem with your biggest client. Or you may find yourself negotiating with someone who holds the highest office in the land.

However formidable your colleague on the other side of the table may be, your objective remains the same—finding a way to meet the other side's needs in a way that also meets your needs. This is the essence of a cooperative approach to negotiation. Let's take a look at a real but complex and unpredictable negotiation that occurred back in 2016 between then Lockheed Martin CEO Marillyn Hewson and then President Donald J. Trump. This negotiation demonstrates the power of understanding the other party's needs and finding creative ways to respond to those needs in a way that accomplishes your objectives.

In 2016, Lockheed Martin struck a deal with the Obama Department of Defense shortly before the election to build another fleet of F-35 fighter planes, which one analyst termed, "the biggest weapons program being funded anywhere in the world."[5] Candidate and later President-Elect Trump publicly criticized the deal, suggesting that he could negotiate a better deal for taxpayers and achieve significant savings over the contract agreed to by his predecessor's administration. As Loren Thompson of the Lexington Institute wrote in *Forbes*, Trump "was not happy with the trillion-dollar price-tag attached to the program for buying over 2,000 planes and then keeping them in operation through 2070."[6]

A series of tweets by Trump starting in November 2016 criticizing both Lockheed Martin and its competitor Boeing over what he viewed as bad deals negotiated by the Obama administration and the companies' expensive costs to build new military and government airplanes sprung Hewson into action.

"The F-35 program and cost is out of control. Billions of dollars can and will be saved on military (and other) purchases after January 20th," Trump tweeted in December 2016.[7]

Facing the incredibly formidable scenario of having to negotiate with someone holding the most powerful office on earth while still meeting the needs of her company, Hewson understood from the beginning that key to the outcome of this was understanding Trump's needs. An in-person meeting with the then president-elect at his Mar-a-Lago Club in Florida couldn't have gone worse. In the days following, more negative tweets about Lockheed and the F-35 were issued. Trump even began publicly promoting a rival aircraft by their competitor Boeing to needle Lockheed.

"Based on the tremendous cost and cost overruns of the Lockheed Martin F-35, I have asked Boeing to price out a comparable F-18 Super Hornet," Trump tweeted in December 2016.[8]

Following this, she hired Trump's former presidential campaign manager Corey Lewandowski to help her better appreciate the president's style and objectives and ultimately steer the discussion toward a favorable resolution for both Lockheed Martin and Trump.[9] A second meeting at Trump Tower in January 2017 reportedly went much better as she and Lewandowski "forged a new, more conciliatory strategy for their discussions with Trump."[10]

As military aircraft analyst Richard Aboulafia put it in an interview with the *Dallas Morning News,* "[Lockheed] realized this isn't a negotiation; this is an exercise in flattery."[11]

As Hewson told *Defense News* in 2017 during the discussions, "if you set aside tweets and look at my interaction, he wanted to first understand the capabilities of the systems and spent time with military leadership understanding the actual programs. And then we had a good dialogue about how do we get through negotiation, how do we continue to bring price down."[12]

"[Trump] recognizes the capability [that] was needed with the F-35, but he also recognized that he wanted to get the best price," she said. "And as a businessman he understands volume and driving costs down. So in that sense I was encouraged by those discussions, and continue to be."[13]

Hewson quickly learned that Trump's needs revolved around his image—portraying an image of Trump as a successful businessman who could negotiate great deals and create American jobs. For example, during her second and subsequent meetings with Trump, she promised to grow the eighteen hundred–person workforce at the Fort Worth, Texas, plant where the F-35 airplanes are assembled.[14]

Even before his tweets, Hewson realized that taxpayer savings would be likely—even absent negotiations with the new administration—because a large order of planes would enable them to scale up production and reduce costs through increased economies of scale. So it wasn't a heavy lift to lower the price and let Trump get a public "win" and burnish his credentials as a successful "negotiator in chief." After all, the bottom line for Lockheed was not one individual contract but increased business far into the future—maintaining existing contracts (even at a lower cost) and securing additional plane orders.

The strategy worked. During his first week in office, Trump was able to announce to reporters that Lockheed had agreed to reduce the costs of building the F-35 by approximately $600 million and also won public praise from the "negotiator in chief."

"When you think about $600 million, it was announced by Marillyn, who's very talented, the head of Lockheed Martin. I got involved in that about a month ago. There was no movement and I was able to get $600 million approximately off those planes."[15]

Ultimately, as Thompson notes, prices fell from the $102 million per plane in the Obama deal to $94 million, "cumulatively saving taxpayers $500 million on just that one production lot." Subsequent deals for additional plane orders brought the price down further to below $80 million. Compared with the final deal negotiated with the Obama Department of Defense, he writes that "the unit cost of the Air Force version is down 27%, the cost of the Marine version is down 27%, and the cost of the Navy version will fall over 30%."[16]

Beyond their initial breakthrough in their relationship that resulted in the revised F-35 contract, Hewson also understood another important need for Trump. To stay in the president's good graces, you needed to be "all in." That meant being a regular participant in advancing the president's policy agenda and continually finding areas to publicly support the White House and laud Trump as a successful leader.

For example, Hewson publicly supported the administration's regulatory reform efforts. By focusing on how regulations drive up production costs, she worked to fashion a win-win scenario in the long run—negotiating significant contract savings with Trump and securing regulatory relief that would drive down costs for Lockheed Martin and their customers going forward.

"Getting rid of regulations that are not adding value, but they're adding costs," she told *Defense News*. "AIA did a study and determined twenty cents on every dollar you spend on military equipment goes toward regulations. Now some of those you need. But some are onerous and unnecessary and inefficient."[17]

Lockheed hosted Trump at its facility in Milwaukee in 2019, where they announced that they were going to increase its workforce by 15 percent.[18] Earlier that year, they reversed plans to close a Pennsylvania helicopter factory after Trump publicly asked them to do so.[19] The company even brought a truck-mounted THAAD anti-ballistic missile system, draped in an American flag, to the White House for a photo op with Trump, where Hewson proudly pitched the firm's American made products with a smiling president by her side.[20] The event was a perfect backdrop to promote the Trump administration's "Made in America" agenda.

At the end of day, her efforts were so successful that a March 2019 *Defense One* headline asked the question—"Has Lockheed Replaced Boeing as Trump's Favorite Defense Firm?"[21]

After a rocky start, Hewson's work to understand Trump's needs ultimately secured the long-term business they were seeking. A true sign of how successful the overall strategy of a woman Trump once mistakenly called "Marillyn Lockheed"[22] came in a public compliment from the president at a White House meeting:

"You know what? You're going to do great and you're going to make more planes. It's going to work out the same, or better," Trump told her.[23]

Hewson's strategy to transition from positions worked brilliantly. Instead of challenging Trump's position of needing to lower the cost of the planes, she sought to understand his interests driving the position. She hired a former Trump staffer to better understand how he works and learned about Trump's desire to secure an early win for the American people as president, his image as a successful businessman and his role as "negotiator in chief." These were all interests she could accommodate so long as she secured a good business deal for Lockheed. To move the business forward, she creatively found a way to discount the airplanes, giving Trump his "win" in exchange for her "win"—maintaining current contracts and additional plane orders far into the future. By transitioning from positions, she connected with what was really driving Trump, and as soon as she satisfied those interests Trump went from an obstacle to an ally in Lockheed's future multibillion-dollar business relationship with the US government.

SAVING MR. BANKS: A CASE STUDY

Let's look at a final case study on transitioning from positions. It is one of my favorite stories about how understanding interests can help us get what we want in business and in life. In 2013 Disney released the movie *Saving Mr. Banks*. It is about the development of the 1964 classic movie *Mary Poppins*.

Saving Mr. Banks stars Emma Thompson as P. L. Travers, the author of *Mary Poppins,* and Tom Hanks as Walt Disney. The movie depicts Travers's tragic childhood in Australia and the two weeks in 1961 when she spent time in Los Angeles meeting with Walt Disney about the rights to her stories.

The movie centers on Travers's negotiation with Walt Disney but flashes back to memories of her childhood. Through those flashbacks, we learn that Travers idolized her fun-loving father, but his alcoholism destroyed the household and eventually caused her mother's attempted suicide. Her father died when she was young, and upon his death, her aunt came to live with her family and eventually became the inspiration for the disciplined and highly proper Mary Poppins character.

A majority of the movie shows Travers completely annoyed at all the ways Disney and his creative team want to tell the story. She eventually gets to a place where she makes ridiculous demands—such as prohibiting the color red from being used in the movie. Disney and his team try time and time again to find a creative direction that is pleasing to Travers but ultimately fail. The tension rises between Disney and Travers, and she leaves to return to her home in London.

Disney and his team take note of Travers's strong objection to how George Banks, the estranged father of the children in the movie, is depicted. He then learns that Travers is a pen name based on her father's name and that her real name is Helen Goff.

At this very moment, Disney understands Travers's interests. He realizes that her objections are not with the creative direction but with how her father is negatively depicted through George Banks. This was not about whether to have animated characters or not. It was about honoring the memory of a father Travers loved and adored.

This leads to the most powerful scene in the entire movie: Disney shows up unannounced at Travers's door in London. He connects with her by talking about his stressful childhood and the challenges he had with his own father. He promises to honor her father and convinces her that telling this story will bring healing to her.

In the end, Travers gives Disney the rights, and the movie ends with her becoming emotional at the premiere as she observes the redemption of George Banks in the film.

What do we learn about negotiation from this story?

Here you have an *issue*: the rights to the story of *Mary Poppins*. We have two positions. Disney wants them. Travers tells him no. Both parties attempt to strengthen their position. Disney invites Travers to Los Angeles and treats her like a queen. He attempts to impress her with the creative direction of the film. Travers wants nothing of it and finds problem after problem with the film as the basis for her refusal to release the rights.

You can see here the problem with a "typical" approach to negotiation. This strategy escalates to a point where there is no deal, the relationship between Disney and Travers has been severely strained, and Disney has spent a ton of time, money, and energy with nothing to show for it.

But Disney is a skilled negotiator. He transitions from positions. He responds to Travers's interests related to her father and is able to get the deal done. As with so many negotiations, both parties' interests are almost completely aligned. Travers wanted to honor her father. Disney revealed a promise he made to his daughter that he would make this movie. For Disney, this wasn't about making money or movies. It was about his relationship with his daughter.

And so here you have a daughter wanting to honor a father and a father wanting to fulfill the wishes of his daughter.

We couldn't have known any of that if we didn't transition from positions. And we might have missed the deal altogether. Having the courage to transition from positions unlocks deals that would not otherwise get done and resolves problems that would not otherwise get resolved.

This is the power of transitioning from positions. By responding to the other party's interests, you also move closer to unlocking another power discussed in chapter 9: empathy.

Build Your Framework—How to Impact Decisions

- Appreciate the role of emotion, ego, and fear in decision-making.
- Take time to build rapport with the other side before diving into the negotiation.
- Ask open-ended questions to get beyond the stated positions.
- Confirm the interests that you believe will affect the other side's decision-making.
- Brainstorm and develop creative solutions that satisfy your interests and the interests of the other side.

Think It Through

- What are the interests that drive the people with whom you negotiate most?
- What are the interests that drive many of your decisions in business and in life?

For more negotiation tools and content,
please visit negotiationmadesimple.com.

CHAPTER EIGHT

THE ROADMAP TO RESOLUTION

Coming together is a beginning; keeping together is progress; working together is success.

—HENRY FORD[1]

Once you understand the value of underlying interests, you'll be eager to explore them in your negotiations with others. I will warn you: these conversations don't happen naturally. This is an area that makes sense intellectually but is difficult to execute practically. But if you can successfully lead others in this direction, you can achieve more than you ever imagined.

The transition from positions is difficult because people sense a loss of control. The negotiation often becomes messy as emotions and personal interests arise in the conversation. The use of positions requires compromise, but the use of interests requires creativity and the integration of new resources. You will find that people are not used to this type of negotiation and, as a result, will seek to avoid it. Therefore, you need a roadmap you can give them to educate them on the process and give them back a sense of control. On the next page is a six-step roadmap for moving away from positions toward interests. I find it useful to get people comfortable with this process before attempting to execute it.

THE ROADMAP TO RESOLUTION

1. Steer the conversation in a new direction.

In negotiation situations such as these, it is not often that people willingly share their cards. They do not bring up their real interests. Instead, they talk about positions. So your first move is to intentionally lead the conversation in a far more productive direction.

I've had people do this with me before. Once, during my time as a university administrator, I called a leadership coach to ask him to come speak to our students. I was ready to jump in and talk about what it would cost for him to come speak, but he slowed us down and changed the conversation. He then asked if we could spend the little time we had on the phone getting to know each other and discussing what we were hoping to achieve through the visit. After five minutes spent learning about each other personally, I found it easier to agree to pay a much higher price than I normally would for a visiting speaker. In those few minutes, he prioritized my interests and those of the students. He creatively responded to those interests. By slowing down and intentionally taking our conversation in a new direction, he was able to secure a handsome fee for his speaking engagement.

2. Ask questions.

One of the most overlooked skills in negotiation is asking questions. Competitive negotiation is about making an offer and trying to convince the other side to accept your proposal. Cooperative negotiation is about working with the other side to explore ideas in search of a solution. This process begins with asking powerful and inspirational questions.

Asking questions is a great negotiator's secret weapon. By asking questions in a negotiation, you can do the following:

- Shift the conversation away from an adversarial give-and-take exchange.
- Build trust and rapport with the other side.
- Discover new information that can unlock a solution.
- Spark innovative thinking and new ideas.
- Put yourself in control of the conversation and the path toward a deal.

For questions to be effective in advancing a cooperative negotiation, they must be asked in a specific way. There's a big difference in how a counselor asks questions and in how an attorney asks questions. You don't want to cross-examine people. You're not looking for one-word answers. You're not looking for agreement or disagreement with a particular statement. You don't want to put people on the defensive, and you don't want to lead them on.

What you really want is the answer to the question "Why?" But you have to be careful in how you ask it. People can get defensive quickly when responding to a question that begins with why. Instead, ask open-ended questions prompting people to tell their story. Use phrases such as:

- Help me understand . . .
- Tell me more about . . .

- Can you talk about . . .
- I'm curious about . . .
- What is it about . . .

The key is to get the other side talking. It's been my observation that when people are talking about themselves, they tend to overshare and will give you information that is valuable to the negotiation without even realizing it. Get them to paint a picture: ask them to give as much detail and information as possible. This is your golden ticket to resolving the problem.

3. Listen.

When people open up, listen. Seems obvious, right? Well, it's not. In fact, listening is one of the most difficult parts of this whole process. The reason listening is difficult is because our brains are smart. While people only speak between 125 and 175 words per minute, we can listen to and process between 400 and 800 words per minute.[2] With that excess capacity, our minds begin to wander. Our body language then signals that we aren't paying attention. The other person begins to suspect we don't care. But that's not the problem: we care, but we let our minds wander.

The solution is focus. Focus on people as they talk and pay careful attention to what they say. In addition, focus on the unstated. Many times it is difficult for people to articulate their interests. For example, it is socially awkward for people to acknowledge their own ego, but that is a major driver in negotiation. People are often hesitant to communicate their fears, but there is an interest at play. With sensitivity, voice the interest for the other side and then ask if you have an accurate understanding of what is driving the other side.

• • •

These first three steps of the Roadmap to Resolution help us gather the interest-based information that we need to progress. The next three steps show us what to do with that information.

4. Create options.

Now it's time to get creative. Brainstorm. Build a list of everything you could do to make the deal come together based on the interests of both sides. Put as many ideas out there as possible. Hold off on evaluation and see where the ideas take you.

Try inviting the other side into this process too. They might come up with some great options. Show them how committed you are to protecting everyone's interests.

One of my favorite ways of stimulating creativity is to get people working together in front of a whiteboard. Have each side develop a list of interests and take time to reflect on the lists. One of the things you will likely notice is that the lists do not clash and in some cases might even be similar. Nevertheless, creativity can work even if the interests are vastly different. Based on this mutual understanding of each other's interests and the common ground realized by examining the lists, you now have a strong foundation from which to pursue a cooperative negotiation. Your job now is to work with the other side and generate creative ideas on how to solve the problem or do the deal in a way that satisfies the interests on that whiteboard.

5. Develop options.

After a solid amount of brainstorming, and hopefully lots of ideas on the table, you can now begin to think critically. Ask yourself, *Which of these ideas are doable?* It will become clear to you fairly quickly which ones are logistically unreasonable or out of reach. At this stage, your goal is to narrow the list to only the ideas that are actually feasible.

This is the moment to get real but not become pessimistic. While dealing with the realities of what is and what is not doable, keep the optimism alive and present in the negotiation. This moment can be the point where people get discouraged and want to give up on the cooperative approach. Your confidence in finding a solution will be key to keeping people engaged in the process.

6. Evaluate options.

Last, ask yourself, *What doable option best meets my interests and the interests of the other side?* Notice the criterion here: not what is best for me or what is best for them, but what is the best option that meets both needs?

If you and the other side can agree upon that, then not only will you have a deal, but you will have a durable agreement that truly solves the problem. You will also have the opportunity to advance the relationship.

It is important to note that the evaluation of ideas comes last in the process. The correct sequencing of steps is vital to the success of the process. If you are like me, you have encountered a colleague who loves to identify and define problems in your organization: breaking down the problem, diagnosing the root cause, and quickly telling everyone who is at fault. What they don't do is offer solutions on how to fix the problems. It's like the doctor diagnosing you with a medical condition but then having no ideas on how to treat it. You need both! What's more, when other people offer ideas on how to solve the problem this colleague is always the first to shoot down the ideas. Eventually, people just stop sharing ideas. As a result, the team suffers because of your colleague's annoying habit of evaluating proposed solutions too quickly in the process.

In cooperative negotiation, the behavior demonstrated by your difficult colleague must be stopped. Proper sequencing of the steps in the Roadmap to Resolution is critical. The evaluation of ideas must happen only after all the ideas are on the table and the ideas that are not feasible have been filtered out. It is only at this point that it is appropriate to begin evaluating which ideas best satisfy the interests of the parties.

This roadmap can be your game changer. It is your guide to engaging the other side in a process that can solve the most challenging problems and help put together the biggest deals. More significantly, this process is also useful for advancing relationships. Cooperative negotiations produce a sense of mutual accomplishment. The intimacy that results from working through this roadmap to put together a deal is helpful to creating healthy long-term relationships with people in your personal and professional life.

Build Your Framework—How to Make the Roadmap to Resolution Work for You

- Decide when the most strategic time in the negotiation is to explore the cooperative approach. Is it at the beginning or after you have reached an impasse in a competitive negotiation?
- Pay attention to the sequencing of the process and don't skip any steps before moving on to the next. The temptation is to begin working to solve the problem before you fully understand it.
- Know that if you are not able to find a solution using the Roadmap for Resolution, you can always return to the competitive approach.

Think It Through

- What problems are you experiencing right now that could benefit from the Roadmap to Resolution?
- Who do you need to educate on this process as a way of strengthening your relationship?

For more negotiation tools and content,
please visit negotiationmadesimple.com.

CHAPTER NINE

THE POWER OF EMPATHY

If you would win a man to your cause, first convince him that
you are his sincere friend.

—ABRAHAM LINCOLN[1]

One of the most powerful cooperative tools used by leaders
today is empathy. Simply defined, empathy is the process of
identifying, sharing, and experiencing the feelings of another
person. In other words, putting yourself in another person's
shoes for a moment. In recent years, empathy has begun to be
recognized as an important business strategy. For example, in
2021, the *World Economic Forum* published an article titled
"Why Empathy Is a Must-Have Business Strategy."[2] The article argues that empathy increases employee loyalty, drives
innovation, and fosters diversity in the workplace. Long before
empathy was recognized as a business strategy, it was identified as a critical negotiation strategy that drove the concept
negotiation scholars call interest-based negotiation. Let's
explore how empathy can help you make negotiation simple.

. . .

A COMMON REACTION TO THE ROLE OF EMPATHY IN NEGOTIATION

As we open the conversation on empathy, I know what you might be thinking: Is it really necessary to get into everyone's feelings, emotions, and personal perspectives as we put this deal together? Too often negotiators, especially in the legal arena, fail to exercise empathy. Instead of directing the conversation toward the interests driving a lawsuit, many lawyers and mediators prefer to keep the conversation focused on the facts, the legal issues, and the money it will take to settle a case. Business leaders can struggle too. Many executives and managers overemphasize hitting metrics, performing to plan, and delivering financial performance. In doing so, they risk failing to understand or steering away from the deeper purpose that drives employee engagement and performance. Neglecting empathy in today's world is perilous to success. Negotiators who exercise empathy in the process will communicate more, know more, and ultimately get more.

HOW EMPATHY CAN LEAD TO SUCCESSFUL NEGOTIATING OUTCOMES

First, it is important to define what we mean by empathy. Harvard Law School professor Robert Mnookin defines empathy as "making an effort to understand your counterpart's point of view in a nonjudgmental way."[3] As business strategist, lawyer, and leading negotiating expert Joseph Campolo cautions—don't confuse sympathy with empathy, which is a common mistake. As he notes, sympathy is when you say, "I understand how you feel. I feel terrible for you." On the other hand, empathy is when you say, "I understand how you feel, and I understand why you feel that way."[4]

As he writes, "The empathetic negotiator understands her adversary's position, but doesn't actually experience it or necessarily agree with it."[5] Rather, he argues, "by tuning into her adversary's emotions instead of just the words, the empathetic negotiator shows that she 'gets it,' which helps the adversary open up and share additional information the empathetic negotiator can use to her advantage."[6] Ultimately, he concludes that "using empathy as a tool to make your adversary keep talking and feel comfortable is key to letting the other side get what *you* want."[7]

Neuroscientific researchers have identified two different types of empathy—affective empathy and cognitive empathy. Two researchers, Marcus Holmes and Keren Yarhi-Milo, explained the difference as that between "feeling and knowing."[8] Affective empathy is the ability of one to comprehend and respond to the emotions of others.[9] Cognitive empathy is the ability to comprehend and understand another's intentions and perspectives.[10]

Empathy is powerful because it often illuminates the path to a deal. As you better understand the needs of the people you are negotiating with, you will know what you need to accomplish in the negotiation to strike a deal. Once that understanding has been established, you can creatively and collaboratively go to work on crafting a deal that is responsive to all the needs on the table. The bottom line—empathy is about listening and learning. And by using empathy strategically, you can drive negotiations to a mutually satisfactory outcome centered on meeting people's needs.

LEAD WITH NEED

Through empathy, your goal is to use what you learn to drive negotiations toward an outcome focused on meeting your needs and your counterpart's needs at the same time. This is what I call the "lead-with-need model," which is based around four core strategies—observe, understand, respect, and solve.

- **Observe**—How do you observe the people you're negotiating with to get a deeper understanding of their needs? Are you interrupting a lot and asserting your position? Or are you listening to what they are saying, asking follow-up questions to learn more information, and conveying through body language, words, and later action that you empathize with their needs?

- **Understand**—How do you understand the people you're negotiating with? You may clearly see across the table that your counterpart is very emotional and talking about a particular concern of theirs or relaying something relevant from their past. Your goal is to get your counterpart to explain as much as possible, to understand both the problem and what is causing them to be emotional.

- **Respect**—Instead of attacking or discrediting through your words, tone, and body language your counterpart's position and feelings, your goal is to show through words and actions that you respect their emotions and perspective. You don't have to agree with it to respect it. By acknowledging it, you can begin to diffuse the adversarial nature of the conversation and begin down a path toward mutual problem-solving.

- **Solve**—Ultimately, this strategy is to build toward reaching common ground and a final solution that both sides will be content with. To do this, you need to use the information that you have gained by observing, understanding, and respecting to establish a connection with your counterpart—building trust and common ground toward a final solution. This is also the moment when you can begin exploring ideas for how to solve the problem based on all that you have learned up to this point about the other side's needs.

By successfully employing the lead-with-need model, you will not only get a real understanding of the needs of your counterpart, but you will transform the posture of the conversation. The whole dynamic of the conversation will pivot from adversaries trying to outmaneuver one another to colleagues trying to solve a mutual problem together. This type of negotiation preserves and, at times, advances relationships.

Take a look at the two images in figure 4. In the first image, you see parties on opposite sides of the table. The posture is adversarial. The parties are working against each other. In the second image, you see the parties on the same side of the table with the problem on the opposite side of the table. Here, the parties are not in total agreement because they are not sitting right next to each other, but they are working together to try to solve the problem. The focus is on overcoming the problem, not beating the other side. In addition, the barriers that divide the parties are removed so the parties can be more collaborative and can more easily communicate. The second image is what the lead-with-need model is all about. Working together to solve problems by finding creative ways to meet everyone's needs.

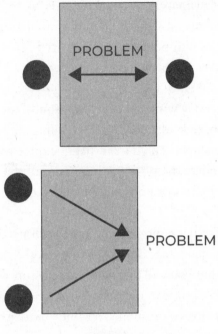

FIGURE 4

What if the second image reflected how you engage colleagues at work? Your business would be more successful. What if the second image reflected how you engage clients or customers? You would have more long-term profitable relationships. What if the second image reflected how you engage your family? You would have healthy family relationships that bless your life. This is the model for getting what we want in life!

FOUR PRACTICAL SUGGESTIONS FOR PROMPTING MORE EMPATHY IN NEGOTIATION

Great negotiators are empathy engineers. Creating an environment for empathy to occur can be difficult and can take time.

Next are four practical suggestions for prompting more empathy in negotiation.

1. Set up the room right.

You may not notice it, but the environment in which you have a conversation can be key to generating more empathy. To illustrate, very few counseling rooms have the patient and the counselor sitting across a table from one another. Instead, these rooms usually have comfortable lounge furniture that sets the stage for open and empathetic dialogue. To cut down the tension in a negotiation, do the same thing. Try sitting in a lounge-style setting—without an imposing conference table and big executive chairs. Sitting on a couch or in more comfortable chairs, or even at a bar table with high chairs, will set the stage for a more relaxed and informal setting. This will hopefully put your counterpart at ease to share with you why they feel the way they do. You might also consider having a whiteboard in the room. This tool can foster ideation and brainstorming, which can help craft the deal or solve the problem.

Holmes and Yarhi-Milo note that "a wealth of evidence suggests that individuals convey their empathic capacity to each other through expressive signaling: the bodily behaviors, unconscious mimicry, and facial microexpression of interpersonal social interaction . . . [which] can help individuals form beliefs about whether the other can empathize."[11]

People tend to conform to their environment and the behaviors modeled by others. This is what I call the law of conformity. If you can create a relaxed environment through your posture and nonverbal behavior, it is more likely others will join you in engaging in a productive conversation about the deal or the problem.

2. Listen well.

How well you listen to your counterpart will largely determine the impact of your empathy. Even if you disagree with the information or perspective being shared, one of the most empathetic statements you can make as a negotiator is, "Thank you for sharing that with me. That is very helpful." I can't recall a single occasion where this phrase was received negatively and didn't lead to a more productive negotiation. People who sense they are being heard will share more and more information, which gives more insights on how to make a deal happen.

3. Find common ground.

Beth Fisher-Yoshida argues that "after bringing down the wall, it is important to find common ground and identify a way forward," by asking questions like "How do you see us moving forward?"[12] She suggests using phrases like "Yes, that could be possible" to move the conversation to an agreeable place.[13] Finding common ground does two major things between negotiators. First, it increases likability. People who like each other are more inclined to do business with each other and say yes to a deal. Second, it provides a foundation on which to construct a deal.

4. Be a learn-it-all negotiator.

You wouldn't expect that you would be able to learn about negotiating with empathy from the CEO of one of the world's largest companies, let alone one in the highly competitive and cutthroat world of technology. A personal tragedy in the life of Microsoft CEO Satya Nadella opened his eyes to the importance of seeing things differently, which ultimately led to a major transformation in the operations of the tech giant he oversees.

Nadella is just the third CEO in the history of Microsoft, following in the footsteps of founder Bill Gates and highly visible and charismatic Steve Ballmer, who would later become the owner of the Los Angeles Clippers basketball team.

He grew up in Hyderabad, India, was raised in a Hindu family, and attended college in both India and the United States before joining Microsoft at age twenty-five.

A few years later, he and his wife, Anu, welcomed a baby boy, Zain, who tragically faced utero asphyxiation while in the womb and was born with severe cerebral palsy, which would require the use of a wheelchair his entire life and constant care from his family. Observing how his wife quickly recovered from a very difficult birth to become a rock of strength for the family was a life-altering lesson for Nadella.

"For Anu, it was never about what this meant for her," Nadella later recalled, "it was always about what it meant for Zain and how we could best care for him."[14]

"Rather than asking, 'why us?' she instinctually felt his pain before her own," he wrote.

"[Anu's] empathy for others runs deep, and from her I have learned that when I infuse empathy into my every day [sic] actions it is power, whether they be in my role as a father or as CEO."[15]

When Nadella was appointed CEO of Microsoft in 2014, he was taking the reins of a tech giant that *Bloomberg News* characterized as a company "enter[ing] middle age."[16]

The company was going through a tumultuous period, as recent acquisitions had not fared well, and competitors like

Apple and Google were surpassing Microsoft for market dominance. The *New York Times* described Microsoft at the time as "a lumbering has-been of the technology world."[17]

Nadella immediately set out to chart a different course. While "his predecessors were notorious for employing tough tactics," Nadella worked to change the corporate culture and restore a "soul" to Microsoft.[18]

"Culture is something that needs to adapt and change, and you've got to be able to have a learning culture," he says.[19]

He was inspired about implementing a learning culture after reading the book *Mindset*, by world-renowned Stanford University psychologist Carol Dweck.

"In there there's this very simple concept that Carol Dweck talks about, which is if you take two people, one of them is a learn-it-all and the other one is a know-it-all, the learn-it-all will always trump the know-it-all in the long run, even if they start with less innate capability."[20]

In the business world, he says adopting a learn-it-all approach can inspire the internal self-reflection that is necessary to pave the way for desired outcomes.

"I need to be able to walk out of [the office] this evening and say, 'Where was I too closed-minded, or where did I not show the right kind of attitude of growth in my own mind?'"[21]

On putting the learn-it-all approach into practice at Microsoft, Nadella writes, "[W]e needed to build deeper empathy for our customers and their unarticulated and unmet needs. It was time to hit refresh."[22]

But don't confuse taking a learn-it-all approach with not being a strong competitor. Nadella recalls an experience playing a cricket match in his native India against an international team that included several Australian players. He recalls that the players were in awe of their opponents, and it showed in their timid performance in the match. An intervention from one of the team officials gave Nadella the proper perspective on learning and competing.

"A business manager of the team saw that I was fielding very far away from the action and just watching. He put me right next to the action, and it was a great lesson to say, 'Look, when you're on the field, you compete. You can have a lot of respect for your competition, but you should not be in awe of them.'"[23]

By adopting a learn-it-all approach at Microsoft, he built upon the tech pioneer's legacy to transform the company to learn to serve the needs of its customers and embrace the future. As the *New York Times* wrote in 2018, "[Microsoft] has fully embraced cloud computing, abandoned an errant foray into smartphones and returned to its roots as mainly a supplier of technology to business customers."[24] During his first four years at the helm, Microsoft's stock price nearly tripled.

When asked what the biggest source of innovation is, surprisingly Nadella replies, "empathy."[25]

He says, "What is the most innate in all of us is that ability to be able to put ourselves in other people's shoes and see the world the way they see it."[26]

Nadella's lesson is great for you as a negotiator.

As a learn-it-all negotiator you will always solve the right problem.

Build Your Framework—How to Learn It All

- Someone observed that God gave us two ears and one mouth for a reason. It's best to use them in that proportion. Listen more than you talk!
- Recognize that empathy is a critical negotiation skill.
- Put yourself in the shoes of the other side to better understand how to craft a deal that works for all.
- Use empathy as your path to influence.

Think It Through

- What are the characteristics of the most empathetic person you know? How can you adopt some of those same attributes?
- What is your observation of the role of empathy in leading people today? Is it becoming more or less important as you do business and navigate today's world?

For more negotiation tools and content,
please visit negotiationmadesimple.com.

Part IV
Deliver the Deal

CHAPTER TEN

PREPARE FOR THE PROCESS

There are no secrets to success. It is the result of preparation, hard work, and learning from failure.

—COLIN POWELL[1]

In 2009, I had the opportunity to travel to China with then Tennessee governor Phil Bredesen as part of an economic development delegation. One day we were on a ninety-minute bus ride to Xi'an to see the Terracotta Warriors, which is a collection of terracotta sculptures depicting the armies of the first emperor of China. Governor Bredesen sat down next to me on the bus. He spent much of the time reading and thinking as we traveled through rural China. Finally, he looked over at me and asked if I was enjoying the trip. That started a conversation that I suspect was just a way to pass the time for him but was a life-changing conversation for me.

I learned two important lessons during that conversation. Graciously, he inquired about what I ultimately wanted to do with my career. I told him that I would like to run a business down the road. In response came the first lesson. Governor Bredesen mentioned how he always had people coming to him asking what they needed to do to advance their career. He joked about how many people wanted his job. He said his advice was always the same: "Do a great job at the job you have now. Don't spend all your time worrying about how to get the next job; just do really well at your current job and it will lead to opportunities to advance your career."

I then asked him about his vision. The governor was a visionary leader who had founded a large health-care company and served as mayor of Nashville before becoming governor. As mayor, he had transformed Downtown Nashville into what it is today. He recruited the Tennessee Titans from Houston, cleaned up Lower Broadway, and created an experience for visitors that makes Nashville one of America's most popular tourist destinations. When reflecting on his vision, he said, "A vision without a plan is just a dream. A leader must be able to see what is to come and have a plan for people to understand how to get there."

As negotiators we all have visions of the great deal. We get excited thinking about what it would mean for our career, the size of our bank account, or our quality of life. Having a vision of a great deal is absolutely necessary because it gives us the motivation to go after it. It is the vision that compels us to move beyond what is comfortable and ask for more. But envisioning the great deal is the easy part. It is delivering it that is hard. As Governor Bredesen teaches us, our vision of the great deal will be only a dream if we do not have a plan. Knowing how to build a plan and mastering the preparation process is absolutely essential to sustained success as a negotiator.

The preparation phase of negotiation is not the exciting part of the process. It is often tedious and becomes stressful as the uncertainty of a negotiation sinks in. This is rehearsal for the actor, training camp for the athlete, or the preflight checks for the pilot. While preparation can take its toll, it is where great deals begin to take shape. It is through disciplined and systemic preparation that negotiators not only discover what a great deal looks like but also begin to form a path toward success.

So, just how much of your efforts should be put in during the preparation phase, you ask? One group of researchers suggests that about 80 percent of your negotiating efforts should take place during the preparation stage.[2] Another group of researchers from the University of Elbasan in Albania caution that you need to be focused in your preparation work, because negotiations are unpredictable, the unexpected will inevitably arise, and having a good negotiation framework is key to guiding your work.[3] It "defines the problem or opportunity," they write, "which involves eliminating irrelevant clutter."[4]

"A framework allows the negotiator to interpret important information through analysis . . . focus[ing] on problems, issues, interests and solutions," they argue. Having a framework "enables senior managers and executives . . . to develop some workable scenarios" to the substantive issues on the table and "focus[es] the team on the results."[5] At the end of the day, they conclude, a framework pushes the negotiation manager to "measure a range of possible outcomes, not just the money."[6]

As part of your preparation process, Northwestern University professor Leigh Thompson recommends asking yourself two very important questions. What do I want? What is my alternative to reaching agreement?[7] The first question requires you to set a realistic but ambitious goal, but Thompson cautions not to set too low a target because you may not feel satisfied if the other party immediately accepts your offer, or too high a target because this may make reaching a deal elusive.[8] A third scenario—where you do so little preparation that you don't know what you want—can end in a variation of the first two scenarios, being either disappointed or suspicious about the other party's good-faith offer.[9]

Once you have determined what you want, it is equally important to prepare for how you will get it. Unfortunately, preparation often focuses heavily on what you want, without much consideration of preparing a strategy for dealing with those you will be negotiating with. Research shows that this is all too common among negotiators.

University of Western Australia, Nedlands, professor Ray Fells conducted a negotiation simulation among graduate students where the participants were instructed to take varying approaches to the negotiation. He concluded from his experiment that although "negotiators tend to give close consideration to what they might achieve, they tended not to give consideration to how they might achieve it."[10] Based on his findings, Fells suggests that more time should be devoted to considering the behavioral aspects of negotiations, rather than simply formulating issue-based strategies.[11] "A second aspect of preparation should be based on the anticipation," he writes, "that if negotiators are taking a positional approach, then the positions may well harden into intransigence and so explicit consideration should be given to behavioural strategies which might forestall a potential deadlock."[12]

You might also think that your preparation is completed once negotiations begin. But Meina Liu of the University of Maryland and Sabine Chai of Western Kentucky University argue that "planning and preparation should go beyond what negotiators should do before preparation" and instead should be considered an ongoing process.[13]

Given that negotiations happen in real time, with lots of unknowns and uncertainties, they make the case that "each time something changes or new information becomes available, negotiators need to update their assessments."[14] They write, "Negotiators may come to the meetings with a rational analysis of possible outcomes. . . . However, many of their aspirations may be thwarted in the encounters with the other party."[15] This means preparation must be done for each round of the negotiation based on the dynamics of the previous rounds.

Let's revisit chapter 6, where we discussed the substance and process of negotiation. You will recall our two big questions:

1. What is the right answer? Substance.
2. How do I get others to the right answer? Process.

What follows is a simple checklist that will prepare you for any negotiation. It is important to allocate time well in advance of a negotiation to work through this checklist and systematically prepare for both substance and process.

As you work through the checklist, you will encounter questions that will require an educated guess. Preparing for a negotiation is about understanding and anticipation. It's like a business plan. You want to think through all the strategic issues, but rarely does a business grow in perfect accordance with its plan. You will find that the value of working through this checklist is not getting it all right but carefully thinking through the issues that will determine your success or failure in the negotiation.

THE NEGOTIATOR'S PREPARATION CHECKLIST

1. Who are the parties to the negotiation?

A party is anyone who will affect or be significantly affected by the negotiation. It includes people who may not be at the table but could become a barrier to a deal. For example, negotiating the dissolution of a marriage will certainly involve the husband and wife as parties, but the kids should be included as parties as well even though they are not named on the pleadings, represented by counsel, or at the table.

2. What are the issues or questions that must be answered to strike the deal or solve the problem?

The issues are the big questions you are trying to answer with the negotiation process. What is the price? How much will it take to settle the case? What will be the salary increase for next year? It should be noted that many smaller subissues will fall under the big issues, but at this stage of preparation the goal is to get the big questions on the table.

3. How important are the issues to you? How important is the relationship with the other party to you?

These questions require you to weigh the value of the issues in the negotiation against the value of the relationship with the other side. The answer to this question will guide your strategy around using a competitive or cooperative approach.

4. Is the other party likely to negotiate competitively or cooperatively?

This question requires a level of anticipation and thinking realistically about how much the other side values its relationship with you. It also prompts you to get ready for a competitive negotiation if that is what you anticipate.

5. How competitive or cooperative do you intend to be during the negotiation?

This question may not have just one answer. For example, you may decide to start cooperatively but be ready to change course to become competitive. The important thing is to be sure you know the game you are playing and respond strategically even if it is uncomfortable.

6. How well do you understand the substance of the negotiation? Is there anything you must learn about the subject matter being negotiated before starting the process?

Knowing the substance is critical to making informed decisions. Do your due diligence and learn about the substance of the negotiation. This may require reading about the subject matter, talking with an informed colleague, evaluating a market, or studying other deals in the same space. At a minimum, you will want to learn the language around what you are negotiating and its value. If the other side picks up on the fact that you don't even know the language of the subject matter, they may be tempted to try to exploit your ignorance. Moreover, I have observed that people rarely just change their minds. Instead, they make new decisions based on new information. Gathering factual information that may help the other side revalue the substance of the negotiation or rethink their position can help steer the deal in your direction.

7. What assumptions are you making going into the negotiation? Do those assumptions need to be tested before the negotiation?

A faulty assumption can kill a deal. It can lead to mismanaged expectations or a potential final deal that just doesn't make sense. Be sure to test your assumptions before proceeding with the process.

8. What alternatives are available to you and the other party if the negotiation is not successful?

It is important to consider what will happen if you are not able to strike a deal. This is not asking what you hope will happen but what could happen if you don't get a deal. Be honest and real as you answer this question.

9. What are the most realistic and likely alternatives for each party? What are the positive and negative consequences of the alternatives for each party?

This is the moment when you distill all of the alternatives into the one that is most likely to occur and analyze it carefully. The answer to these questions will position you to develop a bottom line that is substantively better for you than this likely alternative.

10. What can you do to improve your most likely alternative before the negotiation?

You may have heard of BATNA or your best alternative to a negotiated agreement.[16] The goal here is to increase your leverage in the negotiation by developing a better alternative to a deal. For example, a real estate developer friend of mine was trying to buy a piece of land. The owner was asking way too much for the land. The developer went across the street and bought a similar piece of land. She went back to the owner and informed him that if he didn't come down on price she would build her development across the street. Knowing the real estate developer had a good alternative, he made the necessary concessions on price.

11. What is the most strategic sequencing of the issues in the negotiation?

Conventional wisdom is to start with the smaller issues that will likely not be contentious. The challenge with this approach is that if you get stuck on one of the more difficult issues, there are few options for getting the deal done. Linkage requires a strategic sequencing of issues so if you get stuck on an issue, you will have left room to pull value from another issue to try to reach agreement.

12. What is your ideal outcome of this negotiation?

Knowing your target is the first step toward a more disciplined approach to negotiation. Just like a sharpshooter, you can't hit the target if you can't see it. Taking time to develop your targeted deal will help keep you on track as the process gets tough and the pressure mounts.

13. What is your bottom line?

This is another decision where you will want to be honest with yourself. It is the point to which you will not go unless it means you get a deal. Your bottom line should be a better option than your most likely alternative. Otherwise, just take the alternative.

14. Will you put the first offer on the table or let the other side make the first move?

What is more important to you—influence or information? If it's influence, you should put the first offer on the table. If it's information, you should allow the other side to put the first offer on the table.

15. What will be your opening offer?

Decision time! This is the moment to take all that you have learned about the opening offer and formulate an actual move to start the negotiation. In addition to the substance, consider how you will make the opening offer so it has maximum impact on the expectations of the other side.

16. What does your anticipated dance of concessions look like?

This is your opportunity to map the negotiation. You will not get it exactly right, but there is value in anticipating the process and managing it accordingly.

17. What are the intangible, underlying interests of each party that may affect the negotiation? What is driving each party's decision-making?

It is good to speculate about the other side's underlying interests and carefully think through your own interests. If you are unsure of the other side's interests, develop a strategy to lead a conversation to discover those interests.

18. What creative options might be integrated into the negotiation?

This is the fun part! Time to turn off the analytical part of your brain and let your creative juices flow. Consider all the ways you might satisfy your interests *and* the interests of the other side. At this stage, do not let resources or reality hold you back. Be bold and withhold judgment on the ideas that emerge.

19. What tactics do you anticipate from the other side and how will you deal with them?

This question is especially important if you have previously negotiated with the other side and know the go-to tactics. Develop your game plan to keep their tactics from getting in the way of a great deal.

20. What is the best setting for the negotiation?

This is a situational analysis. Be sure to consider comfort, communication, and convenience. Do not agree to negotiate in a setting that gives the other side a significant advantage.

21. When is the best time for the negotiation?

As the saying goes, "Timing is everything." This is also true in negotiation. Think strategically about negotiating when the other side is most inclined to do the deal you want.

The Negotiator's Preparation Checklist

☐ Who are the parties to the negotiation?

☐ What are the issues or questions that must be answered to strike the deal or solve the problem?

☐ How important are the issues to you? How important is the relationship with the other party to you?

☐ Is the other party likely to negotiate competitively or cooperatively?

☐ How competitive or cooperative do you intend to be during the negotiation?

☐ How well do you understand the substance of the negotiation? Is there anything you must learn about the subject matter being negotiated before starting the process?

☐ What assumptions are you making going into the negotiation? Do these assumptions need to be tested before the negotiation?

☐ What alternatives are available to you and the other party if the negotiation is not successful?

☐ What are the most realistic and likely alternatives for each party? What are the positive and negative consequences of the alternatives for each party?

☐ What can you do to improve your most likely alternative before the negotiation?

☐ What is the most strategic sequencing of the issues in the negotiation?

☐ What is your ideal outcome of this negotiation?

☐ What is your bottom line?

☐ Will you put the first offer on the table or let the other side make the first move?

☐ What will be your opening offer?

☐ What does your anticipated dance of concessions look like?

☐ What are the intangible, underlying interests of each party that may impact the negotiation? What is driving each party's decision-making?

☐ What creative options might be integrated into the negotiation?

☐ What tactics do you anticipate from the other side and how will you deal with them?

☐ What is the best setting for the negotiation?

☐ When is the best time for the negotiation?

Once you have completed the Negotiator's Preparation Checklist, you are ready to fill out the Negotiation Preparation Tool (NPT) (see page 148). This is a sheet you can use to guide you in an actual negotiation or as a way for your team to prepare for a negotiation. You will notice your answers to the questions in the checklist will be the information you need to fill out the NPT. An interactive version of the NPT is available at negotiationmadesimple.com.

Negotiation Preparation Tool

Matter: _____

To download a full-size PDF of the
Negotiation Preparation Tool,
please visit negotiationmadesimple.com.

Parties	Issue(s)	Opening Offer	Fallback Positions	Ideal Outcome	Bottom Line	Most Likely Alternative	Alternatives to a Deal	Underlying Interests	Creative Options
1	2	7	8-10	6	5	4	3	11	12

If you are like me, you may be inclined to glance at the questions on the checklist, think through them a bit, and go for it. Don't! Taking ten to fifteen minutes to thoroughly complete the NPT will be valuable to you as you engage in the negotiation. As part of the strategic-negotiation training I have delivered to thousands of people over the years, participants have the opportunity to negotiate after having worked through a preparation process involving the NPT. My question to them is very simple, "What is it like negotiating with the NPT versus not having the NPT?" The answer is almost always "Easier!"

Below are the five most popular reasons why participants say the NPT makes negotiation easier.

1. You know where you are going and can see a path on how to get there.
2. There are no surprises. You are already prepared for the other side's moves in the negotiation.
3. You are able to drive the cooperative process because you are already thinking about the other side's interests.
4. You are steps ahead of the other side because you can see the big picture of where the negotiation is headed.
5. You are more disciplined at the end and less likely to give away value just to close the deal.

I like to compare the NPT to a football team coaching staff. Some of the coaches are on the sideline and some are up in the press box. The reason for this is perspective. The coaches up in the press box can see things the coaches on the sidelines can't see because they are up high. This perspective enables the coaches to make more strategic decisions when they are calling plays or making personnel decisions. In the same way, the NPT will give you a broader perspective of the deal you are attempting to make. Laying out the process in front of you using the NPT will position you to see potential opportunities or barriers and will give you the insight needed to make strategic decisions that will lead you to a great deal.

Build Your Framework—How to Prepare for a Negotiation

- Make preparation a priority and allow yourself time to fully prepare for the negotiation.
- Work the Negotiator's Preparation Checklist.
- Develop a plan for the negotiation.
- Be committed enough to your plan that you are disciplined, but be flexible enough that you can be dynamic and strategic based on what you encounter in the negotiation.

Think It Through

- Reflect on how you typically prepare for a negotiation. How can you improve your preparation process to produce better outcomes?
- Carefully and comprehensively complete the Negotiator's Preparation Checklist for an upcoming negotiation. How did the completion of this preparation process affect your negotiation effectiveness?

For more negotiation tools and content,
please visit negotiationmadesimple.com.

CHAPTER ELEVEN

OVERCOME THE OBSTACLES

How many wars have been averted by patience and persisting good will!

—WINSTON CHURCHILL[1]

On a normal, wintry mid-January day in 2009, US Airways Flight 1549 took off from New York's LaGuardia Airport at 3:03 p.m., bound for Charlotte, North Carolina.[2] The Airbus A320 plane took off nearly twenty minutes after its scheduled 2:45 p.m. departure time and had 150 passengers and five crew members on board.[3]

As the plane's captain, Chesley "Sully" Sullenberger observed, "January 15, 2009, started just like ten thousand other days literally. Flight 1549 initially like all the other flights for so long was completely routine and unremarkable for the first one hundred seconds."[4] But it would be anything but a routine and unremarkable flight. In fact, the story of Flight 1549 would later be told on countless television programs, and even a Hollywood movie would be made about what happened that day. The passengers and crew didn't know it, but they were about to experience the most traumatic three hundred seconds of their lives.

As Captain Sully tells the story, "This was a large flock of large birds . . . Canada geese. They weigh eight or ten or sometimes twelve pounds. They have five-foot or six-foot wingspans."[5]

"I saw the birds about three football field lengths ahead, but not enough time to maneuver away from them. And then they filled the windscreen as if it were a Hitchcock film," Sullenberger said.[6]

Aviation experts later said that planes like Flight 1549, upon taking off from LaGuardia, would normally be taking off with the plane's nose pointed high in the air, at a speed of nearly 200 miles per hour.[7] This made it a prime target for a massive bird strike, as the pilot would likely not see the birds upon ascent and certainly would have no time to react. "They struck the airplane along the leading edges of the wings, the nose, and into the center—the core—of both jet engines."[8] Copilot Jeffrey Skiles recalls, "Both engines went right back to kind of a hushed state. And that's probably just about as bad as it gets when you're an airline pilot to hear that."[9]

Meanwhile, in the back of the plane, flight attendant Doreen Welsh said she "calmed everyone down. I said, 'It's okay. We might have lost one engine. We'll circle around.' I thought, well everything is okay."[10] But everything was far from okay.

As Captain Sully recalls, "I could feel terrible vibrations I'd never felt in an airplane before. . . . I could smell coming into the cabin air: the burning bird odor from the engines. Then the thrust loss was sudden, complete, symmetrical, bilaterally, both engines at once. It felt as if the bottom had fallen out of our world."[11]

"For over four decades, I had never been so challenged in an airplane that I doubted the outcome," he said.[12]

According to reports, the plane was heading north and reached an altitude of thirty-two hundred feet before the strike occurred.[13] "This is Cactus 1539. Hit birds, lost thrust in both engines. We're turning back toward LaGuardia," he would radio air traffic control.[14] Captain Sully then had only a few seconds to decide where to try and land the plane. "I knew it was only a matter of a few minutes before our flight path intersected the surface of the Earth. I had to choose the best possible place for that to happen," Captain Sully later recalled.[15]

The first option considered was turning back the plane to land at LaGuardia. Captain Sully quickly vetoed this option. "Cactus 1529, if we can get it to you, do you want to try to land runway 1-3?" air traffic control asked him.[16] "We're unable. We may end up in the Hudson," Captain Sully warned.[17] Next, he considered attempting a landing at smaller, nearby Teterboro Airport across the river in New Jersey. He ruled out that option, too, before making the fateful decision to land on the Hudson. "Okay, which runway would you like at Teterboro?" air traffic control asked.[18] "We're gonna be in the Hudson," Captain Sully declared.[19] He later recalled that "the only other place in the entire New York metro area, one of the most densely developed areas in the planet, where it might be possible to even try landing a large jet airliner would be the Hudson River."[20]

Captain Sully then changed the plane's direction west toward the Hudson River, before beginning its rapid descent down the river, while trying to determine how to land the plane. Locked into a course to attempt a water landing on the Hudson River, Captain Sully then had to prepare the stunned passengers and crew members to prepare for landing. He knew that he had to choose his words carefully to convey the seriousness of the situation and ensure all took proper precaution so they could safely evacuate once on the ground. "I wanted to sound confident, not agitated, because I knew that courage can be contagious," he said.[21] "[Brace] signals to the cabin crew, the flight attendants, that an emergency landing is imminent . . . [and] I chose another word to give the passengers and crew in the cabin alike a vivid image . . . of what to expect. We were descending at a pace equivalent to a hotel elevator descending at two floors per second. . . . So I choose the word *impact* to give them that vivid image. I said, 'This is the captain, brace for impact!'"[22] In the cabin, flight attendant Donna Dent said, "We began yelling, 'Brace, brace, heads down, stay down!'"[23] Captain Sully said hearing the flight attendants give their instructions "encouraged me, it comforted me, to know that by saying the few words that I had, but choosing the right words, I had literally gotten my crew on the same page."[24]

He had one more critical action to take before the plane hit the water. As he explains, "The final critical maneuver was for me to try to judge visually looking at the featureless water terrain ahead . . . [because] we were coming down so rapidly that if I misjudged any of them by a fraction, that we might start too soon and get too slow and hit hard, or start too late and descend into the water too rapidly in the wrong altitude."[25]

Passenger Eric Stevenson in seat 12F braced for the final seconds of his life. He told ABC News, "[A]s we were going down, I'm thinking, well, these are the last seconds. I pulled out a business card and I wrote on the back of the business card to my mom and to my sister, I love you. And I shoved it into my pocket, because I thought if the aircraft exploded, at least it would be near my body, and they knew I was thinking of them as we were going down."[26] The plane's course set, Captain Sully steered the Airbus A320 toward impact on the Hudson River.

As described by the *New York Times*, "As stunned witnesses watched from high-rise buildings on both banks [of the Hudson River, the plane] banked left, came downriver, its fuselage lower than many apartment terraces and windows, in a carefully executed touchdown . . . that sent up huge plumes of water at midstream."[27] Flight Attendant Welsh said of the landing, "The back of the plane hit first . . . it was violent, horrible. Things flew out."[28] Her colleague Sheila Dale recalled, "It was a hard impact and I thought, well the gear must not have been down because there was no bounce to it. It was just a slam."[29]

Upon opening the front doors, the aircraft's ramps inflated. In the back of the plane, water began to rush in as the back of the plane was nearer the water surface than the front. "It sounds wonderful to hear your chute opening up . . . there was no pushing and shoving. There was nothing said and there was no eye contact. [The passengers] were just going," flight attendant Donna Dent recalled.[30] Despite some confusion and a little bit of chaos in the back of the plane with the water coming in the plane, all passengers were able to evacuate the plane. Passenger Beth McHugh said, "When the plane hit the water, and the water rushed in the back of the plane, it was frigid cold and that's how I knew I was still alive."[31]

New York Waterway ferries were on the scene within a few minutes to begin evacuating the passengers and carry them to shore. When Captain Sully inspected the plane for the last time, all passengers had been evacuated before he was the final one to leave the aircraft and ferry to safety ashore. A few excruciating hours later, it was confirmed to him that all 155 passengers and crew had indeed survived.

Even though Sullenberger admits that he had never trained for such a scenario, and had only discussed it in theory in a classroom discussion during his flight training, there are a lot of things that he did right on that day.

Several years ago, I had the opportunity to be part of a small group of leaders who met with Captain Sully backstage before a speaking engagement. He took us moment by moment through this harrowing ordeal. We watched the official NTSB video that captured the conversations between Captain Sully and air traffic control. He described the innumerable obstacles he had to overcome to land the plane and bring all the passengers to safety. After hearing Captain Sully reflect on this incident, I believe he got six things right, which led to the "Miracle on the Hudson." These six things are also important lessons for you as a negotiator when facing obstacles to getting a deal.

1. The right approach

The most noticeable thing on the NTSB video is how calm and composed Captain Sully remains throughout the doomed flight. He doesn't get rattled. You never sense any fear in his voice. Emotions don't take over. He remains in complete control of himself and is entirely focused on getting the plane down safely.

Captain Sully's imperturbable approach to this crisis is instructive to negotiators. In negotiation, there will be difficult moments. Parties will walk away from the table. People will seek to deceive you or exert power over you. Personalities and emotions can take over and be difficult to manage. Your job is to be like Captain Sully. In these moments, the best negotiators remain calm and in control. They don't react without thinking. They continue to make strategic decisions and take thoughtful action to overcome the obstacle and get the deal back on track.

2. The right communication

One of the interesting facts about Captain Sully and First Officer Skiles is that the Miracle on the Hudson was their first flight together. Based on their effective communication and interaction, it seemed like they had been flying together for years. Captain Sully attributed their ease of communication to training. He noted how the training took over, which provided an understanding on how they were to communicate with each other. Even though Captain Sully didn't know First Officer Skiles, he knew how to engage him in that moment and how to share information quickly so life-and-death decisions could be made efficiently.

Communication is a critical part of negotiation, especially negotiating through conflict. When you are pursuing a deal, seek to understand how to most effectively communicate with the other side. In addition, when the process grows tense, commit to keeping the lines of communication open. If necessary, get a third party such as a consultant, facilitator, or mediator to help manage the communication. If the communication dies, so does the deal. The best negotiators carefully manage and protect the communication process because they know it is through communication that a deal will get done. Finally, invest in your interpersonal communication skills. Learn active listening and how to communicate with both persuasion and empathy. The better you are at communicating, the easier negotiation will become.

3. The right vision

Seeing the solution in the midst of the problem is part of visionary leadership. This is an important skill for airline pilots and negotiators. One of the reasons all 155 people survived the Miracle on the Hudson was because of Captain Sully's incredible vision. Once he determined he did not have enough altitude and airspeed to make it back to an airport and decided to ditch in the Hudson River, Captain Sully began thinking about where to ditch the plane. He noticed the USS *Intrepid*, an aircraft carrier turned museum located in Manhattan. Captain Sully knew there was a ferry terminal right next to the USS *Intrepid* Museum and figured landing next to that museum would position the ferries to get to the passengers in the shortest time possible. Knowing people would not survive long in the frigid waters, Captain Sully's brilliant vision limited the time people were in the water and saved lives.

Vision is also a trait of highly effective negotiators. They often see the solution or the deal coming together long before others do. They must at times be irrationally confident in pursuing it because skepticism and cynicism can set in during difficult negotiations. Here are three ideas for using vision in negotiation. First, transition your thought process from the problem to the solution. Instead of focusing on the barriers that prevent a deal from happening, look for the opportunities those barriers present. Second, don't give up. Keep working the problem until it is resolved. Simple perseverance is often a winning formula. Finally, recognize that big deals and major conflict may require bold solutions and a big vision. Don't be afraid to think radically about how to get your deal done. Visionary thinking is inspirational and influential. Both of these by-products of vision can make a difference in closing the deal or working out the issue.

4. The right roles

You've probably heard the saying "Do your job!" Whether it is a football coach or your boss at work, this statement reflects the importance of each role on a team. The best results are realized when people do their job and do it well. This was true in the Miracle on the Hudson. Captain Sully's job was to make the decisions. The air traffic controller's job was to find a runway for Captain Sully to land the plane. Unfortunately, there was not a runway close enough to land the plane that day, but the air traffic controller kept trying to find an option for Captain Sully until the very end of the flight and long after it was clear the plane would not make it back to an airport.

As negotiators we must be aware of our role and fulfill that role throughout the negotiation. But there was a moment where Captain Sully's role dramatically changed. By quickly embracing his new role, he helped save lives perhaps including his own. Let me explain. On an aircraft, upon an order from the captain, the crew is responsible for evacuating an aircraft. After Captain Sully landed the plane on the Hudson River and gave the order to evacuate the aircraft, it was the crew that was now in charge. When Captain Sully opened the cockpit door, he came out ready to support the crew and follow instructions instead of directing the crew and giving instructions. This clarity of role led to a highly efficient evacuation of an aircraft sinking into the freezing waters of the Hudson River.

Likewise, to deliver a great deal, negotiators must be dynamic in the roles they fulfill. Matching your role to the moment is the key to overcoming obstacles. Throughout the course of a negotiation, you may need to be a peacemaker, a counselor, a challenger, an adversary, an advocate, a listener, a strategist, a thought leader, a problem solver, an ally, a shark, or a partner. Choosing the right role to accomplish the right task is the strategic decision waiting for every great negotiator.

5. The right values

Captain Sully also teaches us about the importance of values-driven decision-making.

When Captain Sully landed that plane, he took note of the fact that he was no longer the captain of a commercial aircraft but was now the captain of a sinking ship. It is a long-standing maritime tradition that the captain of a sinking ship is always the last to disembark. This meant Captain Sully was the last one out of the airplane that fateful day, which is exactly what occurred.

The values embraced and displayed by Captain Sully in the midst of a life-and-death situation is a great lesson for every negotiator. The values on which you will base your decisions and behavior in the midst of a negotiation must be thoughtfully considered before you find yourself in the heat of the battle. As a negotiator, your values will be tested and challenged. You will be tempted to do things to gain an advantage or obtain a favorable deal. Knowing your values and how they will shape you as a negotiator will enable you to move through those moments and temptations with a sense of confidence and simplicity.

6. The right decision

Finally, the five previous things Captain Sully got right led to the right decision to put the plane down in the Hudson as opposed to trying to make it back to an airport. Captain Sully knew this decision would be challenged after the fact using computer-generated models, but he had to make the decision in the moment with limited information available to him. As the movie *Sully* powerfully depicts, Captain Sully's decision proved to be right, saving the lives of the people on the plane and people on the ground.

Like Captain Sully, negotiators must make consequential decisions in the moment with limited information. To prepare for these moments, the right approach, the right communication, the right vision, the right roles, and the right values are outstanding guideposts that lead to the right decisions.

. . .

The six things Captain Sully got right that led to that miracle landing are a roadmap for overcoming obstacles in the negotiation. In your experience as a negotiator, you will face many obstacles to a deal. In fact, some would argue the negotiation hasn't even begun until both sides have said no to each other and identified the obstacles to getting a deal. While obstacles can be difficult and frustrating, they are also the things that will give you a great sense of victory when you successfully overcome them and strike a deal.

TACTICS

Some of the obstacles you will face as a negotiator will be factual and circumstantial. Others will be personal and psychological. And some will be purposeful and intentional. Tactics are things people do in negotiation to try to gain an advantage. They are designed to influence and they become obstacles to your success. Tactics require a strategy for dealing with them without disrupting the deal.

I've had the opportunity to interview scores of people who negotiate at the highest levels of business, government, and sports. I am always interested in hearing about the tactics people use to get an advantage in a negotiation. I've heard a professional sports executive describe a particular chair he asks the opposing negotiator to sit in: it has a broken-down seat, positioning them low to the ground. Even in his regularly positioned chair, he towers over them, giving himself an edge of intimidation.

I've also seen attorneys set deadlines for their offers and threaten to demand more if the offer is not accepted by that deadline.

These are tactics: strategies used in the midst of negotiations to try to get ahead.

It would be a simpler world if no one used tactics, but you should expect them. Tactics are a usual part of negotiation, but they can become a major barrier to progress if you don't know how to manage them carefully.

You can find a lot of negotiation books and courses that teach tactics. Try a simple Google search: you'll find plenty. In my experience, people pick them up easily and enjoy experimenting with them.

The more difficult, and more important, skill is knowing how to deal with a tactic being used against you.

HOW TO DISARM TACTICS

There are two intuitive ways to respond to a tactic, neither of which are very effective.

The first is to simply ignore it. When people don't know how to deal with a tactic, they usually try this strategy, hoping the other side will simply stop. But contrary to the intended effect, ignoring the tactic usually sends the message that it's working. By trying to ignore the tactics, you inevitably begin playing the other person's game.

Another way people respond is to counter with a tactic of their own. For example, a former colleague of mine went bald early in his adulthood. He tells the story of when he was a young lawyer visiting an opposing counsel's office to engage in settlement negotiations. He arrived at the firm and was escorted to a conference room. After a while, the opposing counsel walked into the room and said, "Well, well, they sent Baldy down to settle this case." Being quick-witted, he replied, "Yes, they did, but they told me not to deal with anyone but the old fat guy. So let's get started."

This tactic is one of personal insults. Each side gave the other a jab. He was clever, but was it the best way to start negotiation? A good exchange of tactics (in this case, personal insults), but perhaps not the best start to a negotiation.

We must be careful not to let tactics get in the way of progress. We can get lost responding to tactics and lose sight of what we are trying to accomplish in the negotiation.

In the end, neither of these approaches really help the end goal of getting a deal. Notice that with each of these, you end up playing the game the other party has chosen. That's not setting you up for success.

Let me suggest an alternative approach, one that keeps you from playing their game. There are three steps: identify the tactic, call it out, and negotiate the process.

1. Identify the tactic.

The first step to managing tactics well is to notice that the other party is using them. Sophisticated negotiators have an eye for tactics: they are looking for them and are ready for them, even if they haven't seen that particular breed before.

Here are a few of the common ones:

- **Bait and switch**: when the negotiator signals that they are willing to do X in order to strike a deal, but once you commit they take it back, requiring even more before commitment
- **Take it or leave it**: when the negotiator becomes unwilling to budge, forcing a decision on you
- **Lack of authority**: when the negotiator has to go check in with another party to get approval and returns with another stipulation
- **Make it personal**: when the opponent attacks you with personal comments, unrelated to the conflict at hand
- **Patronizing**: when the opponent tries to flatter you into an agreement
- **Going in the other direction**: when the negotiator takes a position that moves the parties further away from a deal instead of closer to a deal
- **Creating time pressure**: when a negotiator waits until the last minute, hoping you will concede more because you need the deal within a certain amount of time
- **Physical positioning**: when the negotiator places themselves in a position of dominance, whether that's standing or sitting in a higher chair
- **Bogus demands**: when a negotiator makes demands that they don't really care about but say are really important to them

Whenever your intuition signals there is foul play, stop and pay attention. Is the other party employing a tactic?

2. Call out the tactic.

The next step is to let the other side know that you are aware of the tactic being deployed. This will diminish the impact of the tactic. Call them out on their use of the tactic. Know that by doing so you might create tension in the dynamic as the other side becomes defensive and resents being called out. But in many cases, by simply labeling the tactic, the other side will shut it down, allowing you all to move on to the substance of the negotiation.

3. Negotiate the process.

The power you always have as a negotiator is to simply stop the process. If the other side persists in using tactics, you may determine it is not in your best interest to move forward with the negotiation until the tactic is dealt with. Sometimes you will need to negotiate the *process* before you are in a position to negotiate the substance. Be sure to pursue a deal that eliminates the tactic before responding to any further offers in the process.

I was recently involved in a negotiation in which the other side wouldn't respond to my offers. Instead of providing a counteroffer, the other side would simply state how my offer was not satisfactory to them, and then they would demand we make a better offer. It was a tricky little tactic to get me to bid against myself. Unfortunately, I had a mediator who kept suggesting that I go along with the tactic in an effort to keep the other side engaged. But, by doing so, I would be simply giving away value in exchange for nothing.

In response, I accommodated the mediator's request on one occasion with the warning that I wasn't going to give any further offers without a counter from the other side. On the very next move, the other side tried it again. The mediator came back and told us they were not happy with our offer and wanted a better one. At this point, it was time to shut down the process and stop negotiating until we overcame this tactic. We adjourned for the day and disengaged from the process until we received a counteroffer from the other side. It arrived about two days later, and the negotiation was back on track.

The reality is people will use all kinds of tactics against you. The more familiar you are with them, the faster you'll be able to recognize when it's happening. That awareness is your power. You always have the choice to renegotiate the rules of the dance before moving forward. You don't have to play into their games. You don't have to let the other person's tactics run you over. Start to expect tactics, look for them, and then practice diffusing them.

Build Your Framework—How to Overcome Barriers to a Deal

- Embrace the fact that a multitude of barriers to progress and success will arise in negotiation.
- Be ready to attack them instead of using energy trying to avoid them.
- Take note of what you learn as you encounter barriers. These are outstanding teaching tools.
- Use the three-step approach from this chapter to manage tactics.

Think It Through

- What is a barrier you have encountered in negotiation? How did you deal with it? Would you do anything differently today?
- What is a tactic you have encountered in negotiation? How did you deal with it? Would you do anything differently today?

For more negotiation tools and content, please visit negotiationmadesimple.com.

CHAPTER TWELVE

KNOW THE SECRETS OF SATISFACTION

It's what you learn after you know it all that counts.

—COACH JOHN WOODEN[1]

The great novelist Mark Twain supposedly said, "The two most important days in your life are the day you are born and the day you find out why." I hope this book will launch your new life as a great negotiator, a new birth of sorts. Negotiation is a grand adventure once you develop the confidence to chase your dreams and take on your problems using this process. But before we conclude, let's revisit the why question one last time.

Throughout this book, you have been given knowledge, tools, and ideas. But why? Why will they be useful to you? Why will they give you a competitive advantage in the business world? Why will they make you a better boss, spouse, parent, friend, volunteer, coach, and so on? I believe the answer is, negotiation will help you deliver satisfaction. This is what you are trying to achieve as a negotiator. It is through satisfaction that you will be able to build lasting relationships, loyal customers, and a positive reputation both personally and professionally. To better achieve satisfaction, you must understand it and learn how to use our negotiation skills to deliver it.

THE IMPACT OF PSYCHOLOGICAL SATISFACTION ON NEGOTIATION

Whether a negotiation is successful or not really comes down to psychology—how we consciously (and unconsciously) think and feel about things. If you think about it, everything we discuss in this book involves planning, strategies, and tactics to ensure that who we're negotiating with feels good enough about what we're offering, and how we engage with them, to make a deal.

In an ideal world, we want to get satisfaction out of everything we do and experience, from how good our hair looks in the morning to the jokes Jimmy Fallon tells before we go to bed at night. Not only do we want to be satisfied with everything we do, much of our lives are focused on making those around us satisfied with our interactions and what we have to offer at the workplace, in the community, at home, and in our personal relationships.

Much has been written in media, books, and journals trying to understand the concept of psychological satisfaction in negotiation. You're not going to have to take an online psychology course to learn how to become an effective negotiator. But as a professor and someone who has taught many courses in a college setting about negotiation, I can't resist putting a little academic "meat on the bone." Here I will share some useful insights from some of the world's top psychological researchers that can help you in your effort to successfully appeal to one's inner and outer needs for satisfaction.

Preparation for negotiation is typically quite literal. Driven by facts and data, we aim to create the most lucrative offer that will stand out from the competition. We aim to appeal to one's sense of economic value, or the value that a person places on a good or a service based on the benefit they will derive from it.[2] But as mentioned before, much of negotiation involves more than economics, and is driven by the psychological and the emotional.

Applying the concept of subjective value can help you understand the feelings, perceptions, and emotions involved in a negotiation—and hopefully adapt to this to secure a successful outcome.[3]

There are four components to subjective value, each of which are interrelated:

1. how one feels about their relationships with their counterparts (that is, how strong are the feelings of trust and goodwill toward my counterparts?)
2. how one feels about themselves in the negotiation (that is, how do I feel about my behavior in the negotiations?)
3. how one feels about the negotiation process itself (that is, how fair do I feel the process was?)
4. how one feels about the outcome of the deal[4]

Here's an example that illustrates these four simultaneous thoughts at work: After shaking hands with our counterparts across the table to "seal the deal," the first question we naturally ask ourselves is, how did we do compared to the other side? How you perceive how your competitors feel about the outcome of negotiation can also affect your satisfaction with the deal. In one experiment, researchers falsely told a group of negotiators that their counterpart was happy with the outcome of a deal. They felt less successful about the outcome compared to another group who was told that their counterparts felt disappointed.[5] Ironically, the outcome of the negotiation was the same in both instances.

Other research confirms this notion that individuals can experience more satisfaction when their opponents are disappointed than when they are happy with the outcome.[6] In some cases, knowing that the other guy is disappointed can actually lead to feelings of guilt and more concessions and cooperation.

Both of these examples show that the subjective value we attach to an outcome, not the economic value, is often the key to our feelings of satisfaction.

Researchers who have studied subjective value argue that it may be a desired good on its own, that negotiators may value satisfaction, pride, and connection apart from any economic value that may be achieved in an outcome, or they may value forging a long-term relationship with their counterparts over maximizing short-term gains.[7]

Some of these aspects are things to consider in the "here and now" while negotiations are ongoing. Others are more future-oriented concerns. The bottom line is that one's level of satisfaction from one negotiation, however consciously or subconsciously driven by the individual, can linger and negatively or positively impact potential future negotiations with the same counterpart.

"YOU'VE GOT ME FEELING EMOTIONS"

When thinking about how emotions affect negotiations, I'm reminded of Mariah Carey's 1990s hit song "Emotions."

Researchers have been studying how understanding some of the specific emotions that Carey sings about in her song can affect people's behavior in negotiations. Specifically, they explored how people behave differently when they simply feel emotions versus when they actually express them (typically not in a hit pop song like Carey's).

Take feelings of anxiety, for example. When we feel anxious, our typical subconscious reaction is to leave. Research shows that anxiety can have a significant impact on negotiation, resulting in weak first offers, quick responses to counteroffers, and the increased likelihood to leave negotiations early.[8] But when someone expresses their anxiety in negotiations, it often results in bad outcomes for them as their counterparts take advantage of these feelings to maximize their outcomes.[9] Strategies to help overcome anxiety in negotiation include practice sessions so it seems less intimidating or the use of a third-party negotiator to increase comfort levels.[10]

When we think of emotion in negotiating, we typically think of anger. But overexcitement and overenthusiasm are often present at the negotiating table. High-fiving, "bro hugs," fist pumping, and hooting and hollering can be just as problematic toward securing a positive final outcome than cursing and angry outbursts. This is especially true when thinking about one's subjective value—how you feel about your counterparts and the outcome can negatively affect future negotiations. Overconfidence can also leave you vulnerable to making a bad move. Harvard Business School professor Alison Wood Brooks contends that "the best negotiators achieve great deals for themselves but leave their opponents believing that they, too, did fabulously, even if the truth is different."[11] Her advice—don't let excitement make your counterparts feel like they have lost, and don't let overexcitement give you a sense of overconfidence as it can lead you to make deals based on emotion rather than fact.[12]

Every negotiator would be wise to have awareness of their incidental emotions or feelings that are unrelated to the negotiation.[13] These can include whether it is a sunny day or a cloudy day, whether you are still upset about your favorite team blowing the big game last night, or the drama you're experiencing at home. Having an awareness of these incidental emotions—both your own and those of your counterparts—can help you diffuse them during negotiating sessions. Researchers recommend asking open-ended questions (such as "Terrible game last night, huh?") as a way to let the air out of the tires and get negotiations on a more even keel before moving forward.[14]

"TEXT ME!"

In our increasingly tech-driven world, having a one-on-one meeting seems like a relic of the Cold War era. When my kids connect with their friends, they would never actually call them on the phone. Even email has been kicked to the curb. Rather, they would text them or send a DM (direct message).

In a strange way, the COVID-19 pandemic brought one-on-one or group meetings back to life, albeit virtually. During quarantines and lockdowns, videoconferencing services like Zoom, Skype, and Webex became a way for us to visit with our loved ones and also ensure that our businesses continued to operate while we were stuck at home. As the future of work has accelerated in the waning days of the pandemic—with more and more people working from home permanently, even in cities far apart, videoconferencing has become the norm in the business world, and also in negotiation.

As many of us learned when email became the norm in the workplace, communicating through technology is often complicated, especially where negotiations are involved. It's hard to tell one's intent through words on the page—even if emojis are used. Not being in the room with someone face-to-face can certainly affect levels of satisfaction in negotiations.

Researchers have been looking at whether there are advantages to utilizing technology in negotiations versus face-to-face meetings and how we can secure maximum satisfaction in both parties in an increasingly online world.

A German researcher studied how the communication platform, whether it was a face-to-face meeting or a text-based electronically mediated discussion, influenced satisfaction. Comparing the two, they note that the sequence of how messages are received can be different in a text-based discussion because other messages and distractions can get in the way of discussions, whereas discussions are more focused in a face-to-face meeting.[15] In text communication, senders are likely to review their words more carefully before sending, and texts will surely be reviewed and pondered in more detail than in face-to-face meetings that lead to more spontaneous and emotional reactions.[16] The researchers conclude that those who negotiated over text had lower aspirations though achieved similar economic outcomes to face-to-face negotiations.[17] Texting resulted in more explicit relationship building, however, which led to higher levels of satisfaction. Therefore, you can successfully negotiate using e-mails, texts, or DMs. Select the mode of communication that you believe will set the stage for the best deal.

"REGRETS, I'VE HAD A FEW"

Negotiations are typically about making a choice between one or more alternatives. It's common after making a big decision, especially one involving a lot of money, to have feelings of regret. We may have secured a positive outcome selling one painting for $1,000, but we could have made $10,000 from the art collector if we sold the entire collection.

In the academic world, dwelling on "what could have been" is called an alternate outcome or counterfactual thought.[18] These can be both positive and negative, and they are key to whether one feels psychological satisfaction.[19] When thinking about better possible outcomes that could have been achieved over the negotiated outcome, levels of satisfaction decline. But when one feels like they have "dodged the iceberg" in negotiations and a potential outcome that could have been much worse, feelings of satisfaction increase.

Consider the case of where one side makes an initial offer and the other accepts right away. The one who made the offer should feel happy that their initial offer was accepted, which theoretically meant they got most or all of what they wanted in terms of economic value. Research shows that feelings of regret can materialize even in these cases, as counterfactual thoughts take over about what could have been done better.[20] People felt less satisfied even in cases where there was no material difference in the outcome of a negotiation where an initial offer was accepted versus there being a protracted negotiation.[21]

The prevalence of counterfactual thoughts often increases in negotiations in which the negotiations involved the resolution of multiple issues, finds a group of researchers from Marquette and DePaul Universities. Satisfaction decreased even though the favorable resolution of the often complex discussions increased economic payout, leading the researchers to conclude the irony that negotiators who get the best deals may have the least satisfaction afterward.[22] Their research showed that negotiators who used a computer to aid them in these complex negotiations not only maximized the economic outcomes of the negotiations but were more satisfied with the final outcomes than those who did not.[23]

Having alternatives can often be the key to achieving successful negotiations. But in some cases, an alternative is taken off the table in a negotiation, such as with a time-sensitive offer that expires before the negotiations conclude or with some individual, product, or process no longer being available. In rare cases, there may be no alternatives at all. Negotiators are likely to name a few regrets before discussions even get serious. One group of researchers found that in their experiments in cases with diminished or no alternatives, negotiators tended to be more aggressive in their outlook and initial offers and achieved better results.[24] The reason they were successful, the researchers noted, was that they centered the discussion of their offers on the alternatives that were no longer available.[25] While the negotiation may have ultimately proven successful, psychological satisfaction with the final outcome diminished, even though it was arguably a better outcome, because it was being compared to the alternative that disappeared.[26]

"WE WANT IT ALL"

Until now, we've discussed these concepts of economic value and subjective value as either-or propositions. But, as Freddie Mercury and Queen famously sang, "We want it all." How can we derive more satisfaction from the economic value of the negotiated outcomes while also ensuring that our counter-parts derive satisfaction? A group of researchers suggests that by using a strategy in your discussion to properly frame the negotiation, you can help achieve across-the-board satisfaction.[27] They suggest a conversational strategy that involves "offer framing," or focusing the discussion on their reservation or "bottom line" price.[28] This can be especially useful in so-called distributive negotiations, or those involving very thorny issues when both sides have negotiating positions that are seemingly polar opposites from one another.[29]

Their research found that asking questions like "How does my offer compare to your minimum price?" often leads the other side to think more critically about their "walk away" point. Often it leads them to raise their price and make more favorable counteroffers, which increases feelings of economic value in the final outcome. This leads to increased subjective value and greater feelings of satisfaction.[30]

I am often asked about how to set goals for a specific negotiation. How much should I try to get? When should I say yes? What is a good deal? Like with many things in negotiation, the answer to these questions is always "It depends." One's understanding of the substance of the negotiation, the expectations of a boss or a client, or the market for a product can be helpful in determining an appropriate goal for a negotiation. But as we have discussed at length in this book, there is more to negotiation than just the substance of a deal. What about the relationship with the other side? What about the next negotiation? What about our reputation and what will be said about us online?

In addition, I spend hours in conversations with clients speculating about what the other side will or will not agree to in a negotiation. What is their bottom line? What does a win look like for them? The truth is, we rarely know. While we can get pretty close, this exercise of speculation is not a perfect science. In my experience, I am often surprised both ways. Sometimes the surprise is pleasant, and the other side says yes more quickly than anticipated. Other times, the surprise is frustrating as the other side refuses to say yes even though there is good value on the table by any objective standard.

Our inability to know exactly what we should target in a negotiation or what the other side will do suggests the goal of each negotiation should be something bigger than the substance. The answers to these questions are based on satisfaction, not substance. Satisfaction on both sides of the table should be the target in every negotiation.

The *Merriam-Webster Dictionary* defines *satisfaction* as the "fulfillment of a need or want."[31] It's a simple enough definition, but "needs and wants" covers a lot of ground. Some of our needs are substantive and material: money, a home, a place to work. But many of our needs and wants are physical, personal, psychological, emotional, or even spiritual. When we approach negotiation without taking into consideration all those other wants and needs, it might take us a lot longer to achieve satisfaction. We might fail to reach a deal entirely.

To fulfill all needs and wants in a negotiation requires a dynamic and multifaceted solution.

Don't be overwhelmed: there are three simple categories. Fulfilling satisfaction in each of these three categories will get you well on your way to closing a deal.

THE THREE WAYS TO CREATE SATISFACTION IN ANY NEGOTIATION

1. Process

Before almost every success comes a good process. This is true in business and in negotiation. People want control of their destiny. They will be satisfied with processes that are fair, inclusive, creative, and efficient. How many of us have stopped doing business with a company not because their product was bad but because their level of service was poor or their processes were inconvenient or inefficient? We stop going to a certain grocery store because the lines are always long or the parking lot is always crowded. We quit a membership because the interface is too complicated or the app has glitches.

People expect satisfaction in the process.

2. People

The second area in which to create satisfaction is relationships. People also have a desire to be treated well. The human element is real. I vividly remember my grandfather's death at a hospital near Nashville. He passed away peacefully with his family at his side. It was my job to inform the nurses he had passed. I remember walking down the hall to the nurses' station. I told them what had happened. They said they were going to call the doctor and would be right down. I'll never forget two nurses walking into the room. Before they went to the bedside to pronounce my grandfather's death, they stopped and hugged the three of us in the room. They knew this moment required a human response before a clinical response.

3. Product

Last, people ultimately need some level of satisfaction in the product or how the problem is solved. While product satisfaction is important, many believe it is the single driver of satisfaction. How many of us have had a moment with our customers or our employees or our kids when we ultimately give them exactly what they want and they are still dissatisfied? Unfortunately, many people throw resources at problems to deliver the right product, only to realize that satisfaction with the product is difficult to achieve if there isn't satisfaction with the process or the people.

WHAT TO DO WHEN YOU CAN'T FULFILL ALL THREE

The most effective way to seal a deal is to create satisfaction in all three areas. But what happens if—for whatever reason—you can't deliver in all three areas?

Let me illustrate with a personal story.

A few years ago, my friend and his wife planned a weeklong family trip for their eleven-year-old daughter and nine-year-old son to Disney World. They planned to go from park to park throughout the week. On the second day they were there, the nine-year-old got his foot stuck in a seat belt while getting off a ride. He fell and hit his head and started bleeding a little bit. Thankfully, my friend's son was not injured. Once those at the scene got the bleeding stopped and everything cleaned up, they realized the cut was very small and didn't even require stitches. My friend refused further medical care for his son and his family quickly moved on to the next attraction. Nevertheless,

Disney took the incident seriously and captured my friend's information in a report.

The rest of the day went well. When they got back to their hotel room that evening, they walked in, and they were blown away: there sitting on the bed was a huge stuffed Mickey Mouse. It had a balloon tied around its arm, and sitting down right there in front of this stuffed animal, there was a handwritten note from Mickey. It was a signed picture that said, "To my pal: Hope you're feeling better soon! Love, Mickey Mouse."

I want you to think about that moment for a second: How would that feel for the nine-year-old boy? Who else got a handwritten note from Mickey? I'm sure he was feeling like a million bucks. And because he was feeling great, his parents felt great.

And so what did they do? They went back to Disney World the very next day and spent a whole lot more money.

Let's analyze this story through the lens of satisfaction: Disney did not deliver in terms of product. Their product tripped the nine-year-old, and he bumped his head. So they had to create an alternative plan to deliver satisfaction. Fortunately, they'd already thought through this scenario, and they executed their plan flawlessly. They had a careful process that treated the incident with utmost seriousness, even when it was just a little cut. They also treated the family really well throughout the whole process, even sending a personalized Mickey gift.

When you can't deliver satisfaction in one area, it becomes all the more important to create satisfaction in the other two.

If you can do that, you'll be able to save the negotiation.

Build Your Framework—How to Deliver Satisfaction

- Know the three areas of satisfaction.
- Focus on the areas you can usually control—the process and the people.
- Understand that durable agreements will come only when all the parties are satisfied.

Think It Through

- Reflect on a negotiation when you got the result you wanted but were still dissatisfied. What caused you to be dissatisfied?
- Reflect on an experience that did not go as planned but left you satisfied anyway. How was satisfaction achieved?

For more negotiation tools and content,
please visit negotiationmadesimple.com.

CONCLUSION

Make a Difference One Move at a Time

Sometimes you take it easy and sometimes you make it easy.

—SNOOP DOGG in Corona commercial[1]

In 2006, David Mayer and Herbert Greenberg published an article in *Harvard Business Review* titled "What Makes a Good Salesman."[2] This article didn't draw a lot of attention. It didn't become the basis of a *New York Times* bestselling business book. What it did do is answer a critically important question: "What do the *best* salespeople do differently from the rest?"[3] The answer is not only relevant to becoming a great negotiator, but it is surprisingly simple. The cream of the crop, the best of the best, those that outperformed their peers in negotiating sales transactions, did two things. First, they had more ego drive, which caused them to be more ambitious. Second, they were more empathetic. These two qualities—ambition and empathy—are equally important for negotiators. Even outside the context of sales, ambition and empathy are the keys to using negotiation to produce a more satisfying, impactful, and successful life.

Think about it for a minute. In part II of this book, I asked you to consider the importance of asking for more as a strategy for generating better results in competitive negotiation. This is simply being more ambitious, and as we learned, people tend to be rewarded for their ambition in the negotiation process. Then, in part III, I asked you to lead the process by transitioning from positions and exploring the other side's interests by asking questions and listening. This is empathy at work! Therefore, the whole basis of the *Negotiation Made Simple* approach is ambition and empathy. These are the two characteristics that, when developed, utilized, and balanced appropriately, will make a difference in your negotiations. Add to them the tactical advice in this book and you will become a great negotiator.

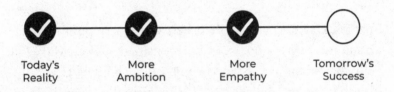

Today's
Reality

More
Ambition

More
Empathy

Tomorrow's
Success

I encourage you to take the skills and strategies learned in this book and go put them to work. After a few weeks of utilizing the Negotiations Made Simple framework, complete the Negotiation Made Simple Self-Assessment on page 191 again. I anticipate you will see substantial growth in your negotiation skills. Use these skills to reach that next level of success! Best of luck in your negotiation adventures!

ACKNOWLEDGMENTS

In 2017, Louie Schwartzberg released a short film called *Gratitude*. The film uses time-lapse videography accompanied by the words of a Benedictine monk to help viewers better appreciate the beauty and blessing that lies within the rhythms of nature. He reminds viewers that everything in life is a gift and that our only appropriate response to the things given to us is gratitude. As I reflect on the many gifts from an array of mentors, colleagues, friends, and family that made this book possible, I am simply filled with gratitude. Your contributions are the essence of this book and the reason why it will see the light of day.

Let me begin by thanking my friend and writing mentor, Don Miller. Your gift was inspiration. Thank you for helping me see myself as an author and for your willingness to include this book as part of Business Made Simple University. I appreciate your friendship more than you could know and look forward to making a difference in the world together through many shared dreams and projects.

I also want to thank my editor and thought partner, Tim Anaya. You were the engine that powered the writing process. Your gift was driving this project to its final destination. I am grateful for how you challenged my thinking and for your insights on how to make this a useful book for readers. Thank you for your wisdom, encouragement, and friendship. You are the best!

I am grateful to Ally Fallon for sitting through an entire course and helping me envision how to turn the content into a book. Your help getting started on this project was invaluable.

I will always be thankful for my publishing and editing partners at HarperCollins Leadership, specifically this book's champion Tim Burgard. This book will make a difference because you believed in it first.

Wes Yoder, you are the best! Thank you for catching the vision of this book and promoting it so effectively. I am honored to have you represent me and will be forever grateful for you guiding me through the process of making this book a reality.

Peter Robinson, our conversation at the Golf Club at Yankee Trace in Dayton, Ohio, in 2007 launched my career in negotiation. You are the one who taught me how to teach negotiation. The doors you opened for me at the Straus Institute for Dispute Resolution at Pepperdine University's School of Law gave me the voice and the platform to write this book. Thank you!

I will always be indebted to my friend, boss, and business partner, Bob Higgins. Your model of leadership is my aspiration. Thank you for the many opportunities you have given me to partner with you in building leaders at Barge Design Solutions and beyond. As I have heard so many people say about you, you are one of the best human beings on planet Earth.

My friends and colleagues at Thrivence and Barge Design Solutions are tremendous partners in the pursuit of helping others be successful. Your intellect, talent, insight, and expertise amaze me. More importantly, the way you care for one another and our clients gives us a unique competitive advantage. Thank you for making it a blast for me to go to work every day.

During an event several years ago, former Tennessee governor Bill Haslam leaned over to me and said, "You hit the jackpot on parents. You are lucky." I couldn't agree with him more. Mom and Dad, your love for people, courageous leadership, and unending grace have changed the world around you. It is an honor to be your son. Thank you for the love and support.

Finally, a loving thanks to my wife, Melissa, and our three children, Weston, Brooklyn, and Deacon. Our adventure through life together is my greatest gift. Thank you for making me such a proud husband and father.

NEGOTIATION MADE SIMPLE SELF-ASSESSMENT

Instructions: Read each statement and consider how often you employ the described behaviors in your negotiations. Indicate your response by circling one of the five numbers that corresponds with your answer. Please be as honest as possible.

	Never	Rarely	Occasionally	Often	Always
1. Before negotiating, you are aware of all the parties and have confirmed who has authority to strike a deal.	1	2	3	4	5
2. Before negotiating, you conduct an analysis of how much you value the issue and how much you value the relationship with the other side.	1	2	3	4	5
3. Before negotiating, you identify the alternatives available to you and the alternatives available to the other side if you do not reach a deal.	1	2	3	4	5

	Never	Rarely	Occasionally	Often	Always
4. Before negotiating, you actively work to improve your alternatives to a deal.	1	2	3	4	5
5. Before negotiating, you establish your target outcome for the negotiation.	1	2	3	4	5
6. You develop a bottom line and stick to it in the negotiation.	1	2	3	4	5
7. You make a strategic decision on whether to be the one who puts the first offer on the table or let the other side put the first offer on the table.	1	2	3	4	5
8. You work through an intentional process to determine your opening offer based on what you want to achieve in the negotiation.	1	2	3	4	5
9. You are ambitious with your opening offer.	1	2	3	4	5
10. You develop a plan for making concessions in the negotiation based on what you anticipate the other side will do in the negotiation.	1	2	3	4	5

	Never	Rarely	Occasionally	Often	Always
11. You adapt your negotiation approach to the approach of the other side.	1	2	3	4	5
12. You are willing to do and say things that are uncomfortable and create tension in the negotiation.	1	2	3	4	5
13. You exercise empathy starting with how you set up the environment for the negotiation.	1	2	3	4	5
14. You ask open-ended questions to explore the interests of the other side.	1	2	3	4	5
15. You look for other resources you can bring into the deal to help get the deal done.	1	2	3	4	5
16. You develop creative options based on the interests of the other side you discover in the negotiation.	1	2	3	4	5
17. You maintain your credibility by ensuring your words, your moves, and your signals are consistent throughout the negotiation.	1	2	3	4	5

	Never	Rarely	Occasionally	Often	Always
18. You identify tactics and address them before proceeding with the negotiation process.	1	2	3	4	5
19. You look for solutions that provide a mutual benefit to both parties.	1	2	3	4	5
20. You pay attention to the process, people, AND problem throughout the entire negotiation.	1	2	3	4	5
21. You walk away if you are unable to get the deal you want or if the other side's negotiation behavior is unproductive.	1	2	3	4	5
GRAND TOTAL *BEFORE* READING *NEGOTIATION MADE SIMPLE*	————————				
GRAND TOTAL *AFTER* READING *NEGOTIATION MADE SIMPLE*	————————				

The Scoring Key (Based on Grand Total)

- You Are a Great Negotiator = 90–105
- You Are Becoming a Great Negotiator = 70–89
- Keep Working and You Will Become a Great Negotiator = 50–69
- You Now Know What It Takes to Become a Great Negotiator = 49 or below

YOUR NEXT STEPS TO MAKING NEGOTIATION SIMPLE

- Embrace your role as a negotiator in business and in life.
- Read *Negotiation Made Simple*.
- Intentionally apply the *Negotiation Made Simple* approach to your negotiations and reflect on your experience.
- Take an online negotiation course—the *Negotiation Made Simple* online course is available through Business Made Simple University (negotiationmadesimple.com).
- Use the Negotiation Preparation Tool (NPT) before each major negotiation. Visit negotiationmadesimple.com to access the tool and take the online instructional course.
- Attend an in-person negotiation workshop with live simulations. The Lowry Group offers live workshops on a regular basis and in-house negotiation training programs (lowrygroup.net).
- Find a mentor with whom you can discuss making deals and resolving problems using the negotiation process.

- Keep a journal of your negotiation successes and be sure to note the skills you used and the moves you made to generate those successes.
- Become a negotiation coach for your friends and colleagues based on your new expertise.
- Enjoy life as a great negotiator!

NOTES

Introduction

1. Simon Sinek, *Start with Why: How Great Leaders Inspire Everyone to Take Action* (New York: Portfolio Books, 2009).

Chapter 1

1. Mike Sager, "What I've Learned: Carrie Fisher," *Esquire*, January 2002, p. 97, https://classic.esquire.com/issue/20020101.

Chapter 2

1. Michael E. Porter, "What Is Strategy?" *Harvard Business Review*, November–December 1996, accessed April 1, 2023, https://hbr.org/1996/11/what-is-strategy.
2. Watch the video at https://www.youtube.com/watch?v=YaooADHwUdM.
3. Merriam-Webster, "Deception Definition and Meaning, accessed April 2, 2023, https://www.merriam-webster.com/dictionary/deception.
4. Harvard Law School Program on Negotiation, "Are Introverts at a Disadvantage in Negotiation?" August 18, 2022, accessed August 28, 2022, https://www.pon.harvard.edu/daily/negotiation-skills-daily/are-introverts-at-a-disadvantage-in-negotiation-nb/.
5. Harvard Law School Program on Negotiation, "Are Introverts at a Disadvantage in Negotiation?"
6. Harvard Law School Program on Negotiation, "Are Introverts at a Disadvantage in Negotiation?"

7. Harvard Law School Program on Negotiation, "Are Introverts at a Disadvantage in Negotiation?"

8. Alice G. Walton, "Trying to Get People to Agree? Skip the French Restaurant and Go for Chinese Food," University of Chicago Booth School of Business, December 11, 2018, accessed August 28, 2022, https://www.chicagobooth.edu/media-relations-and-communications/press-releases/trying-get-people-agree-skip-french-restaurant-and-go-out-chinese-food.

9. Alice G. Walton, "Trying to Get People to Agree? Skip the French Restaurant and Go for Chinese Food."

10. Alice G. Walton, "Trying to Get People to Agree? Skip the French Restaurant and Go for Chinese Food."

11. Rick Page, *Hope Is Not a Strategy: The 6 Keys to Winning the Complex Sale* (New York: The Nautilus Press, 2001).

Chapter 3

1. Dwayne "The Rock" Johnson (@TheRock). "All successes begin with self-discipline. It starts with you. #GrabYourBrassRing." *Twitter,* February 23, 2012, https://twitter.com/TheRock/status/172711897500618752.

2. Kenneth W. Thomas and Ralph Kilmann, *Thomas-Kilmann Conflict Mode Instrument* (Sunnyvale, CA: CPP, Inc., 2002).

3. David A. Lax and James K. Sebenius, *The Manager as Negotiator: Bargaining for Cooperation and Competitive Gain* (New York: Free Press, 1987).

4. Robert Axelrod, "The Volution of Cooperation," adapted from *The Evolution of Cooperation*, Robert Axelrod (New York: Basic Books, 1984), p. 2, https://ee.stanford.edu/~hellman/Breakthrough/book/pdfs/axelrod.pdf.

5. Robert Axelrod, "The Volution of Cooperation."

6. Robert Axelrod, "The Volution of Cooperation."

7. Robert Axelrod, "The Volution of Cooperation."

8. David A. Lax and James K. Sebenius, *The Manager as Negotiator*.

9. Robert Axelrod, "The Volution of Cooperation," p. 6.

10. David A. Lax and James K. Sebenius, *The Manager as Negotiator*.

11. David A. Lax and James K. Sebenius, *The Manager as Negotiator*.

12. Robert Axelrod, "The Volution of Cooperation," p. 5.

13. Robert Axelrod, "The Volution of Cooperation," p. 7.

Chapter 4

1.   William H. McRaven, "Adm. McRaven Urges Graduates to Find
     Courage to Change the World," Speech, University of Texas, Austin,
     May 17, 2014, https://news.utexas.edu/2014/05/16/mcraven-urges
     -graduates-to-find-courage-to-change-the-world/.

Chapter 5

1.   Nancy Solomon, "Solomonism 112," Women Think, accessed April 1,
     2023, www.womenthink.com.
2.   Althea Chang, "The $69 Hot Dog," *The Street*, July 27, 2010, accessed
     November 12, 2022, https://www.thestreet.com/personal-finance/69
     -hot-dog-12806794.
3.   Althea Chang, "The $69 Hot Dog."
4.   Andrej Kras, "12 Examples of Anchoring Bias," insideBE, accessed
     November 12, 2022, https://insidebe.com/articles/12-examples-of
     -anchoring-bias/.
5.   Andrej Kras, "12 Examples of Anchoring Bias."
6.   John S. Hammond, Ralph L. Keeney, and Howard Raiffa, "The
     Hidden Traps in Decision Making," *Harvard Business Review*,
     September–October, 1998, https://hbr.org/1998/09/the-hidden-traps-in
     -decision-making-2.
7.   John S. Hammond, Ralph L. Keeney, and Howard Raiffa, "The Hidden
     Traps in Decision Making."
8.   Ruzana Glaeser, "The Anchoring Effect in Negotiation, and How to
     Eliminate It," *Forbes*, January 31, 2020, accessed November 12, 2022,
     https://www.forbes.com/sites/ellevate/2020/01/31/the-anchoring-effect
     -in-negotiation-and-how-to-eliminate-it/?sh=74f5511d3f34.
9.   Ruzana Glaeser, "The Anchoring Effect in Negotiation, and How to
     Eliminate It."
10. Ruzana Glaeser, "The Anchoring Effect in Negotiation, and How to
     Eliminate It."
11. Harvard Law School Program on Negotiation, "Negotiation
     Techniques: The First Offer Dilemma in Negotiations," September 19,
     2022, accessed November 11, 2022, https://www.pon.harvard.edu/daily
     /dealmaking-daily/resolving-the-first-offer-dilemma-in-business
     -negotiations/.
12. Harvard Law School Program on Negotiation, "Negotiation
     Techniques: The First Offer Dilemma in Negotiations."

13. Harvard Law School Program on Negotiation, "Negotiation Techniques: The First Offer Dilemma in Negotiations."

14. Harvard Law School Program on Negotiation, "Negotiation Techniques: The First Offer Dilemma in Negotiations."

15. Charlene Jimenez, "19 Inspirational Quotes on the Art of Negotiation," *The American Genius*, February 7, 2012, accessed November 12, 2022, https://theamericangenius.com/entrepreneur/19 -inspirational-quotes-on-the-art-of-negotiation/.

16. University of Technology Sydney, "In a Negotiation, How Tough Should Your First Offer Be?" *ScienceDaily*, September 29, 2021, accessed August 28, 2022, https://www.sciencedaily.com/releases /2021/09/210929101857.htm.

Chapter 6

1. Peggy Anderson ed., *Successories: Great Quotes from Great Leaders* (Wayne, NJ: Career Press, 1997), p. 51.

2. Quoteland, "J. Paul Getty Quotes," accessed April 1, 2023, http://www .quoteland.com/author/J-Paul-Getty-Quotes/366/.

Chapter 7

1. Richard M. Nixon, "First Inaugural Address," Washington, DC, January 20, 1969, The American Presidency Project, UC Santa Barbara, https://www.presidency.ucsb.edu/documents/inaugural-address-1.

2. Ryan Pendell, "Customer Brand Preference and Decisions: Gallup's 70/30 Principle," Gallup, September 6, 2022, accessed April 2, 2023, https://www.gallup.com/workplace/398954/customer-brand-preference -decisions-gallup-principle.aspx.

3. Ryan Pendell, "Customer Brand Preference and Decisions: Gallup's 70/30 Principle."

4. Donald Miller, *Building a StoryBrand: Clarify Your Message So Customers Will Listen* (Nashville: HarperCollins Leadership, 2017).

5. Loren Thompson, "Trump Drives Down Price of F-35 Fighter 25% from Obama Level," *Forbes*, June 17, 2019, accessed September 19, 2022, https://www.forbes.com/sites/lorenthompson/2019/06/17/trump -drives-down-price-of-f-35-fighter-25-from-obama-level/

6. Loren Thompson, "Trump Drives Down Price of F-35 Fighter 25% from Obama Level."

7. Tom Benning, "'Cool and Calm': Lockheed's Hewson Turns Trump from Foe to Friend on Fort Worth's F-35," *Dallas Morning News*,

March 28, 2017, accessed September 22, 2022, https://www.dallasnews
.com/news/politics/2017/03/28/cool-and-calm-lockheed-s-hewson-turns
-trump-from-foe-to-friend-on-fort-worth-s-f-35/.

8. Tom Benning, "'Cool and Calm': Lockheed's Hewson Turns Trump from Foe to Friend on Fort Worth's F-35."

9. Kevin Cirilli, "Trump's Ex-Campaign Manager Said to Aid Lockheed in F-35 Dispute," *Bloomberg*, February 2, 2017, accessed September 22, 2022, https://www.bloomberg.com/news/articles/2017 -02-03/trump-s-ex-campaign-manager-said-to-aid-lockheed-in-f-35 -dispute.

10. Kevin Cirilli, "Trump's Ex-Campaign Manager Said to Aid Lockheed in F-35 Dispute."

11. Tom Benning, "'Cool and Calm': Lockheed's Hewson Turns Trump from Foe to Friend on Fort Worth's F-35."

12. Jill Aitoro, "Interview: Lockheed CEO Marillyn Hewson's Review on Donald Trump," *Defense News*, April 5, 2017, accessed September 22, 2022, https://www.defensenews.com/interviews/2017/04/05/interview -lockheed-ceo-marillyn-hewson-s-review-on-donald-trump/.

13. Jill Aitoro, "Interview: Lockheed CEO Marillyn Hewson's Review on Donald Trump."

14. Kevin Cirilli, "Trump's Ex-Campaign Manager Said to Aid Lockheed in F-35 Dispute."

15. Kevin Cirilli, "Trump's Ex-Campaign Manager Said to Aid Lockheed in F-35 Dispute."

16. Loren Thompson, "Trump Drives Down Price of F-35 Fighter 25% from Obama Level."

17. Jill Aitoro, "Interview: Lockheed CEO Marillyn Hewson's Review on Donald Trump."

18. Marcus Weisgerber, "Has Lockheed Replaced Boeing as Trump's Favorite Defense Firm?" *Defense One*, July 23, 2019, accessed September 22, 2022, https://www.defenseone.com/business/2019/07/has -lockheed-replaced-boeing-trumps-favorite-defense-firm/158639/.

19. Marcus Weisgerber, "Has Lockheed Replaced Boeing as Trump's Favorite Defense Firm?"

20. Aaron Gregg, "Trump's 'Made in America' Media Campaign Puts Lockheed Martin in the Spotlight," *Washington Post*, July 23, 2019, accessed September 22, 2022, https://www.washingtonpost.com /business/2019/07/23/with-recent-presidential-stopovers-defense -industry-job-creation-becomes-political-prop/.

21. Marcus Weisgerber, "Has Lockheed Replaced Boeing as Trump's Favorite Defense Firm?"

22. Marcus Weisgerber, "Has Lockheed Replaced Boeing as Trump's Favorite Defense Firm?"

23. Tom Benning, "'Cool and Calm': Lockheed's Hewson Turns Trump from Foe to Friend on Fort Worth's F-35."

Chapter 8

1. Peggy Anderson ed., *Successories: Great Quotes from Great Leaders*, p. 109.

2. Owen Hargie, *Skilled Interpersonal Interaction: Research, Theory, and Practice* (London: Routledge, 2011), p. 200.

Chapter 9

1. Peggy Anderson ed., *Successories: Great Quotes from Great Leaders*, p. 24.

2. Belinda Parmar, "Why Empathy Is a Must-Have Business Strategy," World Economic Forum, October 18, 2021, accessed November 12, 2022, https://www.weforum.org/agenda/2021/10/empathy-business -future-of-work/.

3. Mari Carmen Pizarro, "How to Negotiate Assertively with Empathy," *Forbes*, January 31, 2022, accessed September 22, 2022, https://www .forbes.com/sites/forbescoachescouncil/2022/01/31/how-to-negotiate -assertively-with-empathy/?sh=67a05ed41160https://www.forbes.com /sites/forbescoachescouncil/2022/01/31/how-to-negotiate-assertively -with-empathy/?sh=67a05ed41160.

4. Joseph Campolo, "The Difference Between Empathy and Sympathy in Negotiation (and Why It Matters)," Campolo, Middleton, and McCormick, LLP blog, November 25, 2019, accessed September 22, 2022, https://cmmllp.com/the-difference-between-empathy-and -sympathy-in-negotiation-and-why-it-matters/.

5. Joseph Campolo, "The Difference Between Empathy and Sympathy in Negotiation (and Why It Matters)."

6. Joseph Campolo, "The Difference Between Empathy and Sympathy in Negotiation (and Why It Matters)."

7. Joseph Campolo, "The Difference Between Empathy and Sympathy in Negotiation (and Why It Matters)."

8. Marcus Holmes and Keren Yarhi-Milo, "The Psychological Logic of Peace Summits: How Empathy Shapes Outcomes of Diplomatic Negotiations," *International Studies Quarterly* 61 (2017), pp. 107–122.

9. Marcus Holmes and Keren Yarhi-Milo, "The Psychological Logic of Peace Summits."

10. Marcus Holmes and Keren Yarhi-Milo, "The Psychological Logic of Peace Summits."

11. Marcus Holmes and Keren Yarhi-Milo, "The Psychological Logic of Peace Summits."

12. Marcus Holmes and Keren Yarhi-Milo, "The Psychological Logic of Peace Summits."

13. Marcus Holmes and Keren Yarhi-Milo, "The Psychological Logic of Peace Summits."

14. Satya Nadella, "The Moment That Forever Changed Our Lives," LinkedIn, October 21, 2017, accessed November 16, 2022, https://www.linkedin.com/pulse/moment-forever-changed-our-lives-satya-nadella.

15. Satya Nadella, "The Moment That Forever Changed Our Lives."

16. Dina Bass, "Satya Nadella Talks Microsoft at Middle Age," *Bloomberg Businessweek*, August 4, 2016, accessed November 16, 2022, https://www.bloomberg.com/features/2016-satya-nadella-interview-issue/?leadSource=uverify%20wall.

17. Steve Lohr, "Microsoft Is Worth as Much as Apple. How Did That Happen?" *New York Times*, November 29, 2018, https://www.nytimes.com/2018/11/29/technology/microsoft-apple-worth-how.html.

18. Juana Catalina Rodriguez, "10 Life Lessons from Satya Nadella, Microsoft's CEO About Empathy and Leadership," Medium, March 7, 2022, accessed November 16, 2022, https://medium.com/foundertower/10-life-lessons-from-satya-nadella-microsofts-ceo-about-empathy-growth-and-leadership-a2daa9ecc0c0.

19. Dina Bass, "Satya Nadella Talks Microsoft at Middle Age."

20. Dina Bass, "Satya Nadella Talks Microsoft at Middle Age."

21. Dina Bass, "Satya Nadella Talks Microsoft at Middle Age."

22. Juana Catalina Rodriguez, "10 Life Lessons from Satya Nadella, Microsoft's CEO About Empathy and Leadership."

23. Juana Catalina Rodriguez, "10 Life Lessons from Satya Nadella, Microsoft's CEO About Empathy and Leadership."

24. Steve Lohr, "Microsoft Is Worth as Much as Apple. How Did That Happen?"

25. Adi Ignatius, "Microsoft's Satya Nadella on Flexible Work, the Metaverse, and the Power of Empathy," *Harvard Business Review*, October 28, 2021, accessed November 16, 2022, https://hbr.org/2021/10/microsofts-satya-nadella-on-flexible-work-the-metaverse-and-the-power-of-empathy.

26. Adi Ignatius, "Microsoft's Satya Nadella on Flexible Work, the Metaverse, and the Power of Empathy."

Chapter 10

1. Oren Harari, *The Leadership Secrets of Colin Powell* (New York: McGraw-Hill, 2003).
2. Teuta Balliu and Artan Spahiu, "Pre-Negotiation Activities: A Study of the Main Activities Undertaken by the Negotiators as Preparation for Negotiation," *European Journal of Economics and Business Studies* 6, no. 2 (May–August 2020), pp. 75–86.
3. Teuta Balliu and Artan Spahiu, "Pre-Negotiation Activities."
4. Teuta Balliu and Artan Spahiu, "Pre-Negotiation Activities."
5. Teuta Balliu and Artan Spahiu, "Pre-Negotiation Activities."
6. Teuta Balliu and Artan Spahiu, "Pre-Negotiation Activities."
7. Katie Shonk, "Negotiation Preparation Strategies," Harvard Law School Program on Negotiation Daily blog, July 21, 2022, accessed November 11, 2022, https://www.pon.harvard.edu/daily/business-negotiations/negotiation-preparation-strategies/.
8. Katie Shonk, "Negotiation Preparation Strategies."
9. Katie Shonk, "Negotiation Preparation Strategies."
10. Ray Fells, "Preparation for Negotiation: Issue and Process," *Personnel Review* 25, no. 2 (April 1996), pp. 50–60.
11. Ray Fells, "Preparation for Negotiation: Issue and Process."
12. Ray Fells, "Preparation for Negotiation: Issue and Process."
13. Meina Liu and Sabine Chai, "Planning and Preparing for Effective Negotiation," in *Negotiation Excellence: Successful Deal Making,* Michael Benoliel, ed. (Singapore: World Scientific Publishing, Co., 2011), pp. 15–38.
14. Meina Liu and Sabine Chai, "Planning and Preparing for Effective Negotiation."
15. Meina Liu and Sabine Chai, "Planning and Preparing for Effective Negotiation."
16. Roger Fisher, William Ury, and Bruce Patton, *Getting to Yes: Negotiating Agreement Without Giving In*, 3rd. Revised Ed. (New York: Penguin Publishing Group, 2011).

Chapter 11

1. Winston Churchill, *The Gathering Storm* (New York: RosettaBooks, LLC, 2013; originally published 1948).

2. Ken Belson, "Updates from Jet Rescue in Hudson River," *New York Times* January 15, 2009, accessed October 29, 2022, https://archive .nytimes.com/cityroom.blogs.nytimes.com/2009/01/15/plane-crashes -into-hudson-river/?searchResultPosition=7.

3. Ken Belson, "Updates from Jet Rescue in Hudson River."

4. Chesley "Sully" Sullenberger, Interview, "Captain Sully's Minute-by-Minute Description of the Miracle on the Hudson," *Inc.*, March 6, 2019, https://youtu.be/w6EblErBJqw.

5. Chesley "Sully" Sullenberger, Interview, "Captain Sully's Minute-by-Minute Description of the Miracle on the Hudson."

6. Chesley "Sully" Sullenberger, Interview, "Captain Sully's Minute-by-Minute Description of the Miracle on the Hudson."

7. Ken Belson, "Updates from Jet Rescue in Hudson River."

8. Chesley "Sully" Sullenberger, Interview, "Captain Sully's Minute-by-Minute Description of the Miracle on the Hudson."

9. Jeffrey Skiles, Interview, "Saving 155 Lives," *60 Minutes*, CBS News, February 8, 2009, https://youtu.be/egf93x4-rvQ.

10. Doreen Welsh, Interview, "Saving 155 Lives."

11. Chesley "Sully" Sullenberger, Interview, "Captain Sully's Minute-by-Minute Description of the Miracle on the Hudson."

12. Chesley "Sully" Sullenberger, Interview, "Captain Sully's Minute-by-Minute Description of the Miracle on the Hudson."

13. Ken Belson, "Updates from Jet Rescue in Hudson River."

14. ABC News, "Capt. Sully Reunites with Passengers on 10th Anniversary of 'Miracle on the Hudson,'" *Nightline*, January 16, 2009, https:// youtu.be/IaKPVz8HwHk.

15. Chesley "Sully" Sullenberger, Interview, "Captain Sully's Minute-by-Minute Description of the Miracle on the Hudson."

16. ABC News, "Capt. Sully Reunites with Passengers on 10th Anniversary of 'Miracle on the Hudson.'"

17. ABC News, "Capt. Sully Reunites with Passengers on 10th Anniversary of 'Miracle on the Hudson.'"

18. ABC News, "Capt. Sully Reunites with Passengers on 10th Anniversary of 'Miracle on the Hudson.'"

19. ABC News, "Capt. Sully Reunites with Passengers on 10th Anniversary of 'Miracle on the Hudson.'"

20. Chesley "Sully" Sullenberger, Interview, "Captain Sully's Minute-by-Minute Description of the Miracle on the Hudson."

21. Chesley "Sully" Sullenberger, Interview, "Captain Sully's Minute-by-Minute Description of the Miracle on the Hudson."

22. Chesley "Sully" Sullenberger, Interview, "Captain Sully's Minute-by-Minute Description of the Miracle on the Hudson."

23. Donna Dent, Interview, "Saving 155 Lives."

24. Chesley "Sully" Sullenberger, Interview, "Captain Sully's Minute-by-Minute Description of the Miracle on the Hudson."

25. Chesley "Sully" Sullenberger, Interview, "Captain Sully's Minute-by-Minute Description of the Miracle on the Hudson."

26. Eric Stevenson, Interview, "Capt. Sully Reunites with Passengers on 10th Anniversary of 'Miracle on the Hudson.'"

27. Robert D. McFadden, "All Safe as US Airways Plane Crashes into Hudson River in New York," *New York Times*, January 15, 2009, accessed October 29, 2022, https://www.nytimes.com/2009/01/16 /nyregion/16crash.html?searchResultPosition=9.

28. Doreen Welsh, Interview, "Saving 155 Lives."

29. Sheila Dale, Interview, "Saving 155 Lives."

30. Donna Dent, Interview, "Saving 155 Lives."

31. Beth McHugh, Interview, "Capt. Sully Reunites with Passengers on 10th Anniversary of 'Miracle on the Hudson.'"

Chapter 12

1. Ben Hanback, "What Will You Learn After You Know It All?" *Tennessean*, January 3, 2016, accessed April 1, 2023, https://www .tennessean.com/story/money/2016/01/03/what-you-learn-after-you -know-all/78108188/.

2. Caroline Banton, "Economic Value," *Investopedia*, November 25, 2020, accessed August 27, 2022, https://www.investopedia.com/terms/e /economic-value.asp.

3. Jared R. Curhan, Hillary Anger Elfenbein, and Gavin J. Kilduff, "Getting Off on the Right Foot: Subjective Value Versus Economic Value in Predicting Longitudinal Job Outcomes from Job Offer Negotiations," *Journal of Applied Psychology* 94, no. 2 (2009), pp. 524–534.

4. Jared R. Curhan, Hillary Anger Elfenbein, and Gavin J. Kilduff, "Getting Off on the Right Foot."

5. Jared R. Curhan, Hillary Anger Elfenbein, and Gavin J. Kilduff, "Getting Off on the Right Foot."

6. Konstantina Prassa, Anastassios Stalikas, "Towards a Better Understanding of Negotiation: Basic Principles, Historical Perspective and the Role of Emotions," *Psychology* 11, no. 1 (January 2020), pp.

105–136, https://www.scirp.org/journal/paperinformation.aspx?paperid=97750.

7. Jared R. Curhan, Hillary Anger Elfenbein, and Gavin J. Kilduff, "Getting Off on the Right Foot."

8. Alison Wood Brooks, "Emotion and the Art of Negotiation," *Harvard Business Review*, December 2015, pp. 56–64, https://hbr.org/2015/12/emotion-and-the-art-of-negotiation.

9. Alison Wood Brooks, "Emotion and the Art of Negotiation."

10. Alison Wood Brooks, "Emotion and the Art of Negotiation."

11. Alison Wood Brooks, "Emotion and the Art of Negotiation."

12. Alison Wood Brooks, "Emotion and the Art of Negotiation."

13. Harvard Law School Program on Negotiation, "Emotional Triggers: How Emotions Affect Your Negotiating Ability," August 9, 2022, accessed August 28, 2022, https://www.pon.harvard.edu/daily/negotiation-skills-daily/how-emotions-affect-your-talks/.

14. Harvard Law School Program on Negotiation, "Emotional Triggers: How Emotions Affect Your Negotiating Ability."

15. Ingmar Geiger, "Media Effects on the Formation of Negotiator Satisfaction: The Example of Face-to-Face and Text Based Electronically Mediated Negotiations," *Group Decision and Negotiation* 23 (2014), pp. 735–763.

16. Ingmar Geiger, "Media Effects on the Formation of Negotiator Satisfaction."

17. Ingmar Geiger, "Media Effects on the Formation of Negotiator Satisfaction."

18. Terence T. Ow, Bonnie S. O'Neill, and Charles E. Naquin, "Computer-Aided Tools in Negotiation: The Relationship Between Negotiable Issues, Counterfactual Thinking, and Negotiator Satisfaction," *Journal of Organizational Computing and Electronic Commerce* 24, no. 4 (2014), pp. 297–311, https://epublications.marquette.edu/mgmt_fac/197/.

19. Terence T. Ow, Bonnie S. O'Neill, and Charles E. Naquin, "Computer-Aided Tools in Negotiation."

20. Adam D. Galinsky, Vanessa L. Seiden, Peter H. Kim, Victoria Husted Medvec, "The Dissatisfaction of Having Your First Offer Accepted: The Role of Counterfactual Thinking in Negotiations," *Personality and Social Psychology Bulletin* 28, no. 2 (2002), pp. 271–283.

21. Adam D. Galinsky, Vanessa L. Seiden, Peter H. Kim, Victoria Husted Medvec, "The Dissatisfaction of Having Your First Offer Accepted."

22. Terence T. Ow, Bonnie S. O'Neill, and Charles E. Naquin, "Computer-Aided Tools in Negotiation."

23. Terence T. Ow, Bonnie S. O'Neill, and Charles E. Naquin, "Computer-Aided Tools in Negotiation."

24. Garrett L. Brady, M. Ena Inesi, and Thomas Mussweiler, "The Power of Lost Alternatives in Negotiations," *Organizational Behavior and Human Decision Processes* 162, no. 1 (January 2021), pp. 59–80.

25. Garrett L. Brady, M. Ena Inesi, and Thomas Mussweiler, "The Power of Lost Alternatives in Negotiations."

26. Garrett L. Brady, M. Ena Inesi, and Thomas Mussweiler, "The Power of Lost Alternatives in Negotiations."

27. Michael Schaerer, Martin Schweinsberg, Nico Thornley and Roderick I. Swaab, "Win-win in Distributive Negotiations: The Economic and Relational Benefits of Strategic Offer Framing," *Journal of Experimental Social Psychology* 87 (March 2020).

28. Michael Schaerer, Martin Schweinsberg, Nico Thornley and Roderick I. Swaab, "Win-win in Distributive Negotiations."

29. Michael Schaerer, Martin Schweinsberg, Nico Thornley and Roderick I. Swaab, "Win-win in Distributive Negotiations."

30. Michael Schaerer, Martin Schweinsberg, Nico Thornley and Roderick I. Swaab, "Win-win in Distributive Negotiations."

31. Merriam-Webster, "Satisfaction Definition and Meaning," accessed April 2, 2023, https://www.merriam-webster.com/dictionary /satisfaction.

Conclusion

1. "Make It Easy," Corona beer television commercial, April 6, 2021, accessed April 1, 2023, https://www.youtube.com/watch?v =5I06RXNRk2I.

2. David Mayer and Herbert M. Greenberg, "What Makes a Good Salesman," *Harvard Business Review* 84, no. 4 (2006).

3. David Mayer and Herbert M. Greenberg, "What Makes a Good Salesman."

INDEX

Aboulafia, Richard, 106
accommodation, 35, 37–38
actions, controlling, 16–20
active listening, 157
affective empathy, 123
aggressive first moves, 71–72
alternatives
    choosing among, 176
    to unsuccessful negotiations, 142–43
Anatomy of a Deal, 98–102
anchoring, 64–67, 70
Anderson, George, 4, 5
anger, 173
approach
    of "let's see what happens," 68–69
    for overcoming obstacles, 156–57
assumptions
    in face of uncertainty, 19–20
    questioning your, 17, 21
    testing your, 142
    and trust in intuition, 15–16
avoidance, 35–37
avoiding exploitation, 40–43
Axelrod, Robert, 40–42
Axelrod's Four Steps, 40–42

bait and switch, 164
Ballmer, Steve, 129
Bell's Whisky commercial, 13
bogus demands, 164

bottom line, 143, 178–79
Bredesen, Phil, 135–36
Building a StoryBrand (Miller), 103
buying a car, 51–54, 84–85

Campolo, Joseph, 122
car buying, 51–54, 84–85
Carey, Mariah, 172–73
Chai, Sabine, 138–39
Churchill, Winston, 151
clarity, 42
cognitive empathy, 123
collaboration
    choosing, 35, 39–40
    creating value with, 99, *see also*
        transitioning from positions
comfort
    in making first moves, 67–68
    pursuit of, 11–12, 15
common ground, finding, 128
communication
    through technology, 174–75
    when facing obstacles, 157
competition
    aggressive offers inciting, 71–72
    choosing, 35, 38
competitive negotiation, xiv, 27–28,
        88–91
    to bring about cooperation, 32–33
    in buying a car, 51–54

competitive negotiation (*cont.*)
characteristics of, 47–48
commitment to matching, 32
conceding with purpose in, *see* concessions
cooperative negotiation vs., 27–34
"the dance" in, 52, 56
failure of, 95–98
mastering first move in, *see* opening offers/first moves
need to develop ability in, 50–51
in negotiation scenarios, 36–40
predictability in, 51–57
preparation questions for, 141
recognizing, 29–34
substance and style in, 89–90
using predictability of, 57–58
when to use, 48–50
competitive style, 89–90
compromise, 35, 38–39
concessions, 77–88, 91
in competitive negotiation, 55
creating wins for other side in, 83–84
keeping end in mind with, 81–82
letting the deal come to you in, 82
perception management in, 82–83
preparing for, 144
roles of, 79
saying no to, 84–86
setting up, 80–81
tools for managing, 80
using linkage in, 86–87
conformity, law of, 127
control, sense of losing, 113
conversations
with "lead-with-need model," 125
steering, 114
cooperation, incentivizing, 43
cooperative negotiation, xiv, 27
competitive negotiation vs., 27–34
empathy and creativity in, xiv
in negotiation scenarios, 36–40
preparation questions for, 141
questions in, 114–16
recognizing, 29–34

roadmap to, 113–20
starting with, 41
transitioning from, *see* transitioning from positions
value creation in, 98
cooperative style, 89–90
counterfactual thoughts, 176–77
COVID-19 pandemic, 51, 174
creating time pressure tactic, 164
creativity, xiv, 117
Cuban Missile Crisis, 4–5

daily life, negotiations in, 6–8
Dale, Sheila, 155
"the dance," 52, 56, 70, 166
Deal or No Deal, 9
deception, 14–15
decision making
anchoring affecting, 65–66
based on perceptions, 82–83
ego in, 103–4, 116
emotion in, 102–4
with limited information, 160–61
for negotiation strategy, 34–36
regrets about, 176
uncertainty in, 13–16
values-driven, 160
Dent, Donna, 154, 155
difficult people, 49
Disney, 109–10
Disney, Walt, 110–12
Disney World, 181–82
distributive negotiations, 178
Dweck, Carol, 130
dynamics in negotiation, 29–34

economic value, 171, 172, 176–78
ego, as decision driver, 103–4, 116
emotions
in decision making, 102–4
feeling vs. expressing, 173
with first offers, 67
incidental, 174
and satisfaction, 172–74
tuning in to, 123
when facing obstacles, 156–57

"Emotions" (song), 172–73
empathy, xii, xiv, 121–32
   defined, 121, 122
   "lead-with-need model" of, 124–26
   power of, 122–23
   reaction to role of, 122
   suggestions for prompting, 126–31
   types of, 123
end goal, when making concessions,
   81–82
ethics in negotiating, 14–15
expectations management, 70, 72–83
exploitation, avoiding, 40–43
extroverts, 18, 19

Fallon, Jimmy, 170
Fells, Ray, 138
first moves, xiv. *see also* opening offers
Fishback, Ayelet, 19
Fisher, Carrie, 3
Ford, Henry, 113
forgiveness, 41–42
formidable people, 104–9
fraud, 14–15
Frohlinger, Carol, 67

Gates, Bill, 129
getting played, avoiding, 74–76
Getty, J. Paul, 83
Glaeser, Ruzana, 66
going in the other direction tactic, 164
great negotiators
   characteristics of, xii, 185–86
   as empathy engineers, 126
   lives of, xii–xiii
   self-awareness of, 17–18
   strategic skills of, xiii–xv
Greenberg, Herbert, 185

Hammond, John S., 66
Hanks, Tom, 110
hard things, doing, 12–13
Hewson, Marillyn, 104–9
Holmes, Marcus, 123, 127
HOPE, xv–xvi
Hope Is Not a Strategy, 21

if, as linkage in concessions, 87
information
   in building strategy, 21–22
   limited, in decision making, 160–61
insulting offers, responding to, 69–70
intangible factors, 98
interests in negotiations, 100–102
   identifying, 144
   positions vs., 101–2
   understanding and responding to,
      104–9, *see also* Roadmap to
      Resolution
introverts, 18–19
intuition, 15–16
issues in negotiations, 111, 137–40, 143

Johnson, Dwayne "The Rock," 25

Keeney, Ralph L., 66
Kennedy, John F., 4, 5
Kilmann, Ralph, 34

lack of authority tactic, 164
law of conformity, 127
Lax, David, 40
"lead-with-need model," 124–26
learn-it-all negotiators, 128–31
"let's see what happens" approach, 68–69
letting the deal come to you, 82
Lewandowski, Corey, 106
Lincoln, Abraham, 121
linkage, in making concessions, 86–87
listening
   active, 157
   with empathy, 128
   in Roadmap to Resolution, 116–17
Liu, Meina, 138–39
Lockheed Martin, 104–9
lying, 15

make it personal tactic, 164
The Manager as Negotiator (Lax and
   Sebenius), 40
Mary Poppins, 109, 110
Mayer, David, 185
McHugh, Beth, 155

McNamara, Robert, 4, 5
McRaven, William H., 47, 49
meals, sharing, 19
Mercury, Freddie, 177
Microsoft, 128–31
Miller, Don, 13, 103
Mindset (Dweck), 130
"Miracle on the Hudson," 151–61
Mnookin, Robert, 122
moves in negotiation
    as signals, 31, 32
    substance of, 31

Nadella, Anu, 129
Nadella, Satya, 128–31
needs of others
    "lead-with-need model," 124–26
    understanding and responding to,
        104–9, *see also* empathy
    see also interests in negotiations
Negotiation Made Simple
    Self-Assessment, xv, 191–95
Negotiation Preparation Checklist,
    140–47
Negotiation Preparation Tool (NPT),
    147–50
negotiation(s), 3–10, 197–98
    becoming a professional in, 8–10
    in daily life, 6–8
    defined, 3
    dynamics of, 29–34
    exciting nature of, 9
    outlining your, xvi–xv
    recognizing situations as, 4–6
    uncomfortable feelings in, 12
negotiation strategy, 25–44
    and avoiding exploitation, 40–43
    cooperative vs. competitive, 27–34,
        see also competitive negotiation;
        cooperative negotiation
    deciding on, 34–36
    and dynamics of negotiation, 29–34
    evaluating scenarios for, 36–40
    and voices in your head, 26–27
The Negotiator, 9
negotiator(s)

great, *see* great negotiators
learn-it-all, 128–31
satisfaction of, 177
seeing yourself as a, 3–10
New York Times, 131, 155
Nixon, Richard, 95
NPT (Negotiation Preparation Tool),
    147–50

offer framing, 177–79
opening offers/first moves, xiv
    anchoring in, 64–67
    avoiding blunders with, 64–72
    avoiding getting played with, 74–76
    capturing influence with, 72
    comfort vs. strategy in, 67–68
    in competitive negotiation, 61–76
    in "the dance," 52–53
    extreme vs. reasonable, 72–83
    firm vs. soft, 73
    insulting, 69–70
    "let's see what happens" approach
        with, 68–69
    positioning for concessions with, 80
    power of, 69
    preparing for, 144
    purpose of, 70–71
    responding to, 73–74
    strategic questions about, 72–73
    too aggressive, 71–72
opportunities, xii
options
    creating, 117
    developing, 117–18
    evaluating, 118–19
    preparing ideas for, 145
overcoming obstacles, 151–67
    disarming tactics for, 162–66
    in "Miracle on the Hudson," 151–61
    right approach in, 156–57
    right communication in, 157
    right decision in, 160–61
    right roles in, 159–60
    right values in, 160
    right vision in, 158–59
    tactics for, 161–62

overconfidence, 173–74
overexcitement, 173–74

parties to negotiations, 140
patronizing tactic, 164
perceptions
    and leaving room for concessions,
        80–81
    managing, 82–83
    of value, 171–72
physical positioning tactic, 164
Porter, Michael, 11
positions
    in Anatomy of a Deal, 99–100
    in competitive negotiation, 55
    defined, 99
    interests vs., 101–2
    to set up concessions, 80
    transitioning from, see transitioning
        from positions
Powell, Colin, 135
predictability, in competitive
    negotiation, 51–58
preparation phase, 135–50
    efforts taking place during, 137
    Negotiation Preparation Checklist,
        140–47
    Negotiation Preparation Tool, 147–50
    as ongoing process, 138–39
    questions to ask during, 137–38
process
    negotiating the, 165
    satisfaction with, 180
product, satisfaction with, 181
psychological satisfaction, 79, 170–72,
    177. see also satisfaction

Queen, 177

Raiffa, Howard, 66
Reagan, Ronald, 15
regrets, 176–77
Roadmap to Resolution, 113–20
    asking questions in, 114–16
    creating options in, 117
    developing options in, 117–18

evaluating options in, 118–19
    listening in, 116–17
    sequencing of steps in, 118–19
    steering conversations in, 114
Robinson, Peter, 83
roles, when facing obstacles, 159–60
room setup, 127

satisfaction, xv, 169–83
    and counterfactual thoughts, 176–77
    defined, 179
    and durability/repeatability of deals,
        84
    and emotions, 172–74
    with how people are treated, 180
    offer framing for, 177–79
    in only two of three areas, 181–82
    with the process, 180
    with the product, 181
    psychological, 79, 170–72
    and technology, 174–75
Saving Mr. Banks, 109–12
saying no to concessions, 84–86
SEAL training, 49
Sebenius, James, 40
self-assessment, xv, 191–95
self-awareness, xiii–xiv, 17–23
self-management, xiii–xiv
    four questions for, 20–22
    seeing yourself as a negotiator, 3–10
    strategy for, 11–23
Serendipity, 65
setting for negotiations
    room setup, 127
    situational analysis of, 145
sharing meals, 19
Shark Tank, 9
signals
    of empathic capacity, 127
    negotiating moves as, 31, 32
    responding in kind to, 41
Sinek, Simon, xv
Skiles, Jeffrey, 152, 157
Snoop Dogg, 185
Solomon, Nancy, 61
Starbucks, 102

Start with Why (Sinek), xv
steering conversations, 114
Stevenson, Eric, 154–55
strategy
    controlling your actions, 16–20
    and doing hard things, 12–13
    in first moves, 67–68
    for negotiation, *see* negotiation
        strategy
    for self-management, 11–23
    and uncertainty, 13–16
    and your intuition, 15–16
styles, competitive vs. cooperative,
    89–90
subjective value, 171–73
substance of negotiations, 31, 89–90,
    141–32
Sullenberger, Chesley "Sully," 151–61
Sully, 161
sympathy, empathy vs., 122–23

tactics, 161–66
    anticipating, 145
    calling out, 165
    collaborative approach as, 99
    disarming, 162–66
    identifying, 163–64
take it or leave it tactic, 164
target deal, 81–82, 143
technology, satisfaction and, 174–75
Tennessee Department of
    Transportation (TDOT), 7–8
tension
    from calling out tactics, 165
    in competitive negotiation, 56–57, 89
text, negotiating over, 175
Thirteen Days, 4–5
Thomas, Ken, 34
Thomas-Kilmann Conflict Mode
    Instrument, 34–36
Thompson, Emma, 110
Thompson, Leigh, 137–38
Thompson, Loren, 105, 107
thoughts, counterfactual, 176–77
Thrivence, 103–4
timing of negotiations, 145

transitioning from positions, 95–112
    and Anatomy of a Deal, 98–102
    case study on, 109–12
    and emotion in decision making,
        102–4
    with formidable people, 104–9
    power of, 102–3, 112
    sense of loss of control in, 113
    see also Roadmap to Resolution
treatment of people, satisfaction with,
    180
Trump, Donald J., 104–9
trust
    assumptions about, 20
    establishing, 42
    and intuition, 15, 16
    and too much competition, 33
Twain, Mark, 169

uncertainty
    in decision making, 13–15
    instinct and assumptions in face of,
        19–20
    and intuition, 15–16
    overcoming, 22–23

values, 36, 160
vision
    ideas for using, 158
    plans for reaching, 136–38
    when facing obstacles, 158–59
voices in your head, 26–27

Walesa, Lech, 77
Welsh, Doreen, 152, 155
"What Makes a Good Salesman" (Mayer
    and Greenberg), 185
"Why Empathy Is a Must-Have Business
    Strategy," 121
"why," finding the, xv–xvii, 115–16, 169
wins
    creating perception of, 80–83
    for other side, creating, 83–84
Wooden, John, 169

Yarhi-Milo, Keren, 123, 127

ABOUT THE AUTHOR

John Lowry is a recognized authority on negotiation through his experience as a lawyer, business consultant, entrepreneur, settlement counsel, and university administrator. His results-focused, systematic approach to negotiation has been successfully implemented by thousands of professionals across the United States. He regularly serves as a settlement counsel representing clients in complex litigation matters. John teaches negotiation at the top-ranked Straus Institute for Dispute Resolution at Pepperdine University's School of Law and in Vanderbilt University's Master's in Management in Health Care program.

John serves as the president of Thrivence, a management consulting firm affiliated with Barge Design Solutions in Nashville, Tennessee. In addition to leading the firm, John counsels clients on strategy, revenue growth, leadership development, and conflict management. He also serves as president of The Lowry Group, LLC ("TLG"). At TLG, he provides negotiation training and coaching for governmental entities, major insurance companies, health-care organizations, and other businesses.

In 2016, John was selected by Harvard Business School to participate in its Young American Leaders Program. In addition, he has served as a California State Assembly fellow. John earned his bachelor's degree in speech communications from Pepperdine University and his master's degree in religion from Abilene Christian University. He received his juris doctorate degree from Southern Methodist University's Dedman School of Law. He has also completed graduate work in dispute resolution at the Straus Institute for Dispute Resolution at Pepperdine University's School of Law and in public policy at California State University, Sacramento.

John resides in Nashville with his wife, Melissa, and their three children.

If you learn better via video, binge-watch John Lowry's course Negotiation Made Simple on the Business Made Simple platform at BusinessMadeSimple.com.

HOW TO

Grow Your Small Business on Autopilot

6 Proven Steps to Higher Revenue, Less Chaos, and More Freedom

Business Made Simple

Get a free checklist with six proven steps to experience higher revenue and more freedom in your business. Download the checklist at BusinessMadeSimple.com/GrowNow.